Welcome to the

2004

This edition has been researched and written
by
Anna Anthony

 Thank you for helping Great Ormond Street Hospital Children's Charity in 2004, the centenary of the first ever production of Peter Pan.

The rights of Peter Pan were bequeathed by JM Barrie to GOSH. The value of this fantastic legacy remains a secret, at Barrie's request, in keeping with the magic and mystery of Peter Pan.

Through the sales of these guides we will have raised over £30,600. Since 1998 we have contributed to the funding of a mobile X-ray unit, syringe pumps, infusion pumps and a hoist, but this year we are committed to helping with a much bigger project tackling the hospital infrastructure. This 10-year redevelopment programme will upgrade the Hospital and increase its overall size enabling treatment for over 20% more patients. In the pursuit of excellence, the plan will bring the hospital right up to date with modern day medical practices and clinical care.

Funds contributed in 2004 will go towards the first stage of the re-development. A brand new Patient and Accommodation Centre, opening in 2004, will include 30 rooms for children who require short-stay treatments, along with their families. It will also contain eight transitional care flats for children who are well enough to leave their wards but need some care before they are allowed to return home.

We are proud to announce that a 6p contribution to the above charity will be made for each 'Let's Go with the Children' book sold this season. Thank you for your support. Registered charity No. 235825 ©1989 GOSHCC. ☆ 2003 GOSHCC

Getting yourself involved

Great Ormond Street Hospital Children's Charity needs everyone's support as they aim to raise over £20 million each year. There are many ways to get involved from trekking in Namibia to attending musical concerts. Log on to www.gosh.org or call 0207 916 5678 for an up to date listing of planned events, some of which can involve the whole family. Look out particularly for special Peter Pan themed events throughout the year.

Published by **Cube Publications**, 290 Lymington Road,
Highcliffe, Christchurch, Dorset BH23 5ET
Telephone: 01425 279001 Fax: 01425 279002
www.cubepublications.co.uk
Email: enquiries@cubepublications.co.uk
2nd edition
ISBN 1 903594 38 3

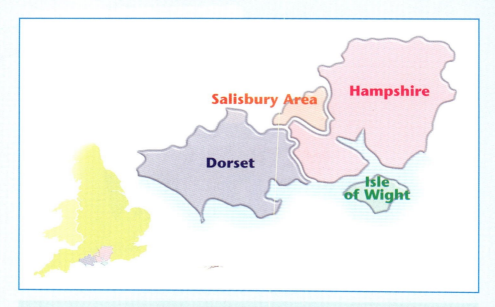

How to use this guide

This guide is one of a set of 13 covering all the counties of England and each county in this edition is colour coded as shown on the map above.

There are several chapters of subject interest as listed in the Contents opposite enabling you to choose something specific for you and your children to do or somewhere for you all to go.

If you have young children who love animals, dip into the Farms, Wildlife & Nature Parks chapter, or, if you have active teenagers, take a look at the Sports & Leisure chapter where you will find something to keep them busy.

Check out History, Art & Science and widen young horizons or choose a nearby venue from the Free Places chapter. A surprising number of things are free.

Whatever your budget, plan a day out to include a variety of activities. You may like to hire a boat, take a train ride, visit a really interesting museum, go bowling, stop off at a soft play centre, try snow sports, visit a zoo or go for a hike. Whatever interests you and your family, there is information included within the following chapters to help you occupy a wet afternoon, a long weekend or the whole school holidays.

We have highlighted price bands, facilities for school trips, places that are open all year and places that cater for birthday parties, but please call in advance if you have special needs or want particular information.

Whether you live locally or you are just visiting, you will find an amazing wealth of diverse interests, entertainments and activities in this area for children of all ages. We hope you will discover more about the area than you thought you already knew.

Please write to us with any constructive comments on the guide. We shall be delighted to hear from you. Our address is on page 1.

Use this guide with a good geographical map to help you find your way. Discover somewhere new, plan your route and keep the children busy by encouraging them to help with the navigating.

Contents

How to use the guide	2
Useful Information	4
Trips & Transport	7
Adventure & Fun	13
History, Art & Science	21
Sports & Leisure	31
Free Places	41
Farms, Wildlife & Nature Parks	49
Places to Go Outside the Area	59
London	61
Index	67

Key

Price codes are given as a maximum entry cost for a family of four, (2 Adults, 2 children):
A: £10 **B**: £20 **C**: £30 **D**: £40 **E**: £50 **F**: FREE **G**: Over £50 **P**: Pay as you go

Schools — School party facilities, visits by arrangement
Birthdays — Birthday parties are organised here
NT — National Trust property - www.nationaltrust.org.uk
EH — English Heritage property - www.english-heritage.org.uk

Telephone Numbers are provided for most entries.
Should you require special facilities for someone with a disability, please call before your visit to check suitability.

Opening Times

LAST ADMISSIONS
Many last admission times are an hour before the quoted closing time. If in any doubt, phone and ask if you know you will be arriving late. Don't get caught out and be disappointed!

WINTER AND CHRISTMAS OPENING
Many attractions close earlier in Winter and most are closed over Christmas and New Year. If you want to visit in this period, call in advance to check! At the time of going to print not all opening times were decided. We have suggested you phone for opening times if this was the case!

The contents of this publication are believed to be correct at the time of going to print. The publishers cannot accept responsibility for errors or omissions, or for changes in the details given and the publishers cannot accept responsibility for the conduct or behaviour of any establishment or company featured in this guide. Every best effort has been made to ensure the accuracy and appropriateness of information, but the publishers urge the reader to use the information herein as a guide and to check important details to their own individual satisfaction with the bodies themselves.
Published by Cube Publications.
Printed by Southbourne Printing Co Ltd. Artwork by Ted Evans Design.
© 2004 Maureen Cuthbert and Suzanne Bennett.
All rights reserved. No part of this publication may be reproduced by printing, photocopying or any other means, nor stored in a retrieval system without the express permission of the publishers.

USEFUL INFORMATION

LARGE ENTERTAINMENT VENUE
DORSET: Bournemouth: Bournemouth International Centre Exeter Rd 01202 456400.

LOCAL COUNCILS
The Local Councils have Leisure Services Departments looking after a wide range of leisure facilities, many of which are featured within this guide, from the best parks and open spaces to sports facilities and museums. They may be able to provide further information on special events and playschemes organised for children, particularly in the school holidays.

DORSET: Dorset County Council: 01305 251000. Bournemouth 01202 451451. Christchurch 01202 486321. East Dorset 01202 886201. North Dorset 01258 454111. Poole 01202 633633. Purbeck 01929 556561. West Dorset 01305 251010. Weymouth & Portland 01305 838000.

HAMPSHIRE: Hampshire County Council: 01962 841841. Basingstoke 01256 844844. East Hants 01730 266551. Eastleigh 023 8068 8000. Fareham 01329 236100. Gosport 023 9258 4242. Hart 01252 622122. Havant 023 9247 4174. New Forest 023 8028 5000. Portsmouth 023 9282 2251. Rushmoor 01252 398398. Southampton 023 8022 3855. Test Valley 01264 368000. Winchester 01962 840222.

SALISBURY AREA: Salisbury 01722 336272.

ISLE OF WIGHT: Isle of Wight 01983 820000.

Rushmoor Borough Council Leisure Services, www.rushmoor.gov.uk 01252 398000, covers Aldershot and Farnborough in Hampshire and boasts a wide range of leisure facilities, with a good mix of indoor and outdoor sites. These include an outdoor lido with picnic areas, a golf course, snowsports centre, bowling, indoor play facilities, museum, indoor swimming, gymnastics academy, and arts and entertainment venues. Rushmoor lies in an area of great natural beauty with the River Blackwater and Basingstoke Canal meandering through, providing great places for outdoor activities such as cycling, walking, watching wildlife and canoeing. A comprehensive programme of events is available, including Victoria Day in July, the Army Show in July, the fireworks spectacular on the first Saturday in November, the Princes Hall pantomime for all ages and SNAP discos, suitable for 11-16 year olds.

TOURIST INFORMATION CENTRES
Tourist Information Centres are a great complement to this guide and can provide advice and detail on the many interesting local events that take place and local accommodation for visitors, as well as stocking colour leaflets about many of the attractions featured in this guide.

DORSET: Blandford Forum 01258 454770. Bournemouth 0906 802 0234. Christchurch 01202 471780. Dorchester 01305 267992. Poole 01202 253253. Shaftesbury 01747 853514. Swanage 01929 422885. Wareham 01929 552740. Weymouth 01305 785747. Wimborne Minster 01202 886116.

HAMPSHIRE: Aldershot 01252 320968. Alton 01420 88448. Andover 01264 324320. Basingstoke 01256 817618. Fareham 01329 221342. Fleet 01252 811151. Fordingbridge 01425 654560. Gosport 023 9252 2944. Havant 023 9248 0024. Lymington, Lyndhurst and New Forest 01590 689000. Petersfield 01730 268829. Portsmouth 023 9282 6722. Ringwood 01425 470896. Romsey 01794 512987. Southampton 023 8022 1106. Winchester 01962 840500.

SALISBURY AREA: Amesbury 01980 622833. Salisbury 01722 334956.

ISLE OF WIGHT: Cowes Newport Ryde Sandown Shanklin Ventnor Yarmouth General Information Line for all towns: 01983 813800/813818.

Please mention this guide when visiting attractions.

Look what you can do!

Longdown Activity Farm p51

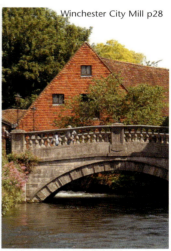
Winchester City Mill p28

Paultons Park p17

Swanage Railway p11

Monkey World p50

Spot the difference...

& see just some of the great places you can go by bus along the South Coast

Combined bus travel & entrance tickets are available to a number of the South's top attractions, including...

- BUTLINS
- ISLE OF WIGHT
- PORTSMOUTH HISTORIC DOCKYARD
- WEALD & DOWNLAND OPEN AIR MUSEUM

day goldrider £5.70 Adult
£4.20 Child/Senior
£11.40 Family

one days unlimited bus travel on Stagecoach services throughout the South East

buy from your driver

Stagecoach

for further info
0845 121 0170

www.stagecoachbus.com

See Portsmouth Harbour from the water

The trips leave regularly from Easter to September, for 1 hour tour with commentary. During the trip you will see historic harbour fortifications, HMS Warrior, HMS Victory, The Naval Base, ships of the Royal Navy including aircraft carriers when in harbour, the Continental Ferry Port, large ferries, commercial docks plus views of Porchester Castle, the Solent sea forts and the Isle of Wight.

Trips leave from the beach landing stage, Clarence Esplanade, Southsea (next to Hovercraft).

J. Butcher & Sons Ltd.
Tel: 023 9282 0564 Fax: 023 9287 4666
Email: bbt@blueboattrips.com
14 Broad Street, Portsmouth, Hants PO1 2JE

It is a real adventure for children to go on a journey and to experience other forms of transport, either as an organised excursion or trip or trying out other vehicles for themselves. You can hire boats or bicycles, take bus trips, ride steam trains or land trains, cruise waterways and simply enjoy getting away from the family car!

BICYCLE HIRE

Boat hire facilities may be closed out of season.

DORSET
Poole, Coolcats Leisure, Sandbanks Hotel, Sandbanks, (seasonal), 01202 701100.
Swanage, Bikeabout, High Street, 01929 425050.

HAMPSHIRE
Beaulieu, Forest Leisure Cycling, main car park, National Motor Museum, 01590 611029.
Brockenhurst, Country Lanes Cycle Centre, Railway Station, 01590 622627. **Cycle Experience,** Island Shop, Brookley Road, 01590 624204.
Burley, Forest Leisure Cycling, Village Centre, 01425 403584.
Fordingbridge, Country Lanes Cycles, Sandy Balls Holiday Centre, 01425 657907.
Lyndhurst, AA Bike Hire New Forest, Gosport Lane, 023 8028 3349.

SALISBURY AREA
Salisbury, Hayball Cycle Sport, 26-30 Winchester Street, 01722 411378.

ISLE OF WIGHT
Freshwater, Bikemech, 11 Regina Road, 01983 756787 (private house, ring in advance).
Ryde, Battersby Cycles, 2 Hill Street, 01983 562039.
Shanklin, Offshore Sports, Orchardleigh Road, 01983 866269.
Yarmouth, Isle Cycle Hire, The Square, 01983 760738.

BOAT HIRE

DORSET
Bournemouth, Durley Chine. Rowing boats. Tuckton Tea Gardens. Motor boats and rowing boats.
Christchurch, Christchurch Quay. Motor boats and rowing boats.
Swanage, Swanage Bay. Canoes, motor boats and pedaloes.
Wareham, Wareham Quay. Rowing boats.
Weymouth, Weymouth Beach. Pedaloes.

HAMPSHIRE
Andover, Charlton Lakeside Pavilion. Pedaloes.
Basingstoke, Eastrop Park. Pedaloes and rowing boats.
Lymington, Seawater Pool, Bath Road. Canoes and rowing boats.
Odiham, Basingstoke Canal. Canoes and rowing boats.
Petersfield, Heath Lake. Canoes and rowing boats.
Riseley, Wellington Country Park. Pedaloes and rowing boats.
Southsea, Canoe Lake. Pedaloes.

SALISBURY AREA
Salisbury, The Afon Bar, Millstream Approach, 01722 552366. Rowing boats.

ISLE OF WIGHT
Ryde, Waterside Boating Lake, Esplanade. Pedaloes and canoes.
Shanklin(near), Dunroamin Beach. Canoes.

BOAT TRIPS & FERRY SERVICES

DORSET

Bournemouth Pier, The Dorset Belles, www.dorsetbelles.co.uk 01202 558550. During the season, trips linking Bournemouth, Poole, Brownsea Island, Swanage and the Isle of Wight. Cruises through the Dorset lakes, along Purbeck coast, and sunset and firework cruises.

Poole, Brownsea Island Ferries, 01929 462383. Trips from the Quay to Sandbanks and round the islands of Poole Harbour, Mar-Oct. *Schools*.

Sandbanks, Brownsea Island Ferries, 01929 462383. Trips to Poole and Brownsea Island, Mar-Oct. *Schools*.

Southbourne, Bournemouth Boating Services, Tuckton Bridge, 01202 429119. Trips to Wick Ferry, Christchurch Quay and Mudeford Beach, Easter-Oct. *Schools*.

Weymouth Harbour, White Motor Boats, 01305 813246. Trips to Portland Castle, Easter-Oct. *Schools*.

HAMPSHIRE

Basingstoke Canal. Navigate from Greywell, Hants, to the River Wey Navigation at New Haw. Tearoom open Wed-Sun, picnic benches and play area at Canal Centre, Mytchett. Phone 01252 370073 for information.

Beaulieu River. Operating from Bucklers Hard (entry Price C) trips go down river and there is a commentary on places of interest. Tours run every hour, operating 11.30am-4pm in low season and 11.30am-5pm in high season. Available Easter-Oct. Call 01590 616203. *Price A*.

Gosport, Gosport Ferry, 023 9252 4551. A ferry service operates daily from 5.30am to midnight, linking Gosport and The Hard and Portsmouth. Cruises also available from here, May-Oct. *Schools*.

Keyhaven, Hurst Ferries, 01590 642500. There are hourly services to Hurst Castle, afternoon cruises to Needles lighthouse and a ferry to Yarmouth, Isle of Wight. Ferry runs Easter-mid Oct. A limited service operates in Winter. *Schools*.

Lymington, Wightlink Isle of Wight Ferries, 0870 582 7744. A car and passenger service which takes about 30 minutes to reach Yarmouth, Isle of Wight. *Schools*.

Odiham, Surrey and Hampshire Canal Cruises Ltd, 01962 713564. Public and charter trips on a traditional style narrow-boat are organised Easter-Oct. Special rates for schools. *Schools Price G*.

Portsmouth, P & O Ferries, 0870 2424 999. Treat the children to the thrill of a sea crossing to either Le Havre or Cherbourg in France or to the Port of Bilbao in Spain.

Wightlink Isle of Wight Ferries, www.wightlink.co.uk 0870 582 7744, operate three routes to the island with car ferries from Portsmouth or Lymington and a high-speed passenger service from Portsmouth Harbour to Ryde Pier Head. The beaches on the island are ideal for families. Whether you seek fun days or choose to relax at quieter spots, there is a place for everyone, and you could be there in just 15 minutes with Wightlink. Attractions on the island range from places of historical interest such as Osborne House, which was once Queen Victoria's residence, to many different types of animal centres where you can see horses, parrots, flamingos and otters. Travel back in time with the Wax Works, or enjoy bygone days on the Isle of Wight Steam Railway. These are just a taste of the delights awaiting visitors to the island. The choice is endless. Please telephone for more information on any of Wightlink's services, or for a copy of their 'Day Trips' leaflet. (Special Saver Fares for a car and 4 people.) *Schools* Check out outside back cover.

Southampton, Red Funnel Ferries, 023 8033 4010, run a passenger-only Red Jet hydrofoil from the Town Quay to Cowes, a journey lasting 25 minutes. A vehicle and passenger ferry, which takes one hour to do the same journey, leaves from the Royal Pier.
White Horse Ferries Ltd, Hythe Ferry, Town Quay, 023 8084 0722. A regular ferry service to Hythe Pier in Southampton Water. **Schools**.

Southsea, Blue Boat Trips, 023 9282 0564, provide an ideal opportunity to see a wide range of exciting activities in Portsmouth Harbour by water. The trips operate regularly from Easter-Sept, for one hour tours with commentary. You will see historic harbour fortifications, HMS Warrior, HMS Victory, the Naval Base, Warships of the Royal Navy (including aircraft carriers when in harbour), the Continental Ferry Port, large ferries, Commercial Docks, Rat Island, Submarine HMS Alliance, and views of Portchester Castle, the Solent sea forts and the Isle of Wight. Special trips for school parties and groups can be arranged at any time of the year. It is essential for large parties to book in advance when group discounts will be made available. Trips leave from the beach landing stage, Clarence Esplanade, Southsea (next to the hovercraft). Services subject to weather and other circumstances. **Schools Price B Check out page 6.**

Hover Travel, Clarence Esplanade, 01983 811000. The hovercraft takes only ten minutes to take foot passengers to Ryde on the Isle of Wight.

ISLE OF WIGHT

Alum Bay, Needles Pleasure Cruises, Beach Jetty, 01983 754477. Cruise to view the Needles at close range! A regular service runs Easter-Oct, 11am-4.40pm (weather permitting), with trips every half an hour during July and August. **Schools Price B**.

Fishbourne, Wightlink Isle of Wight Ferries, Car Ferry Dock, 0870 582 7744. Day return service to Portsmouth. A half-hourly service all year, more in Summer season. **Schools Open all year.**

Ryde, Hover Travel, Hovercraft Terminal, 01983 811000. Frequent service to Portsmouth and Southsea Hoverport, taking approximately ten minutes. **Schools Open all year Price C**.
Wightlink Isle of Wight Ferries, Pierhead, 0870 582 7744. Foot passengers day return to Portsmouth, a half-hourly service all year, more in Summer season. **Schools Open all year.**

West Cowes, Red Funnel Ferries, Fountain Quay, talking timetable 0870 444 8889. This is a non-bookable, walk-on, high-speed catamaran service running approx every half an hour to Southampton. **Schools Open all year Price D** (day return).
Solent and Wightline Cruises, 01983 564602. Cruises to the Needles or Portsmouth operate all year round. **Schools Open all year Price D**.

Yarmouth, Dorset Belles, Yarmouth Pier, 01202 558550. Summer cruises from Yarmouth Pier to the Needles operate on selected days, Apr-end Aug. Possible day return to Bournemouth planned. Phone for further information. **Schools Price B**.
Hurst Ferries. Cruises to Hurst Castle, Keyhaven, Alum Bay and the Needles operate daily, Jun-Sept, 01590 642500. Phone for information. **Schools Price B**.
Puffin Cruises, Yarmouth Harbour. Ferry trips to Lymington town quay, 01590 644004. Daily service mid Jul-end Aug, phone for Sept-mid Jul schedule. Also cruises to the Needles, May-Sept. **Schools Price C**.
Trips in ex-lifeboat to Needles, Hurst Castle and Western Solent, 01983 753989. **Schools Price C** (per hour).
Wightlink Isle of Wight Ferries, 0870 582 7744. Car and passenger ferry to Lymington, a half-hourly service all year, more in Summer season. **Schools Open all year.**

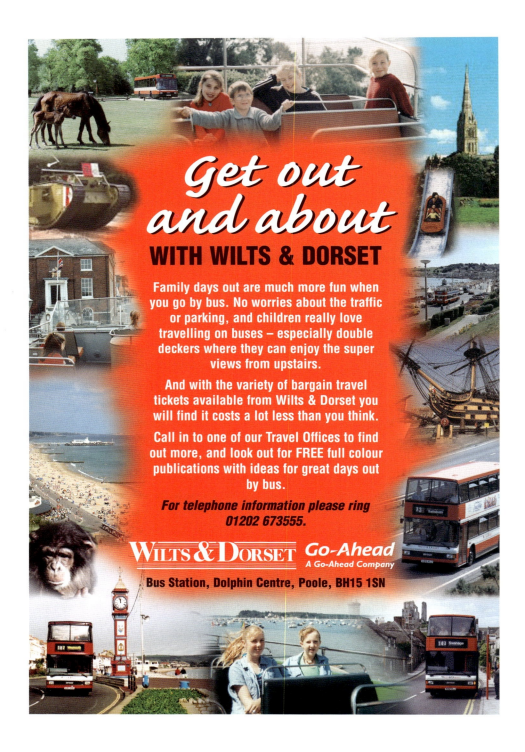

BUS TRIPS

DORSET

Wilts & Dorset Buses. Get out and about this Summer and enjoy the many sights and sounds around with Wilts & Dorset Buses. There is plenty to see and do; shops, beaches, museums or just visiting friends. It is cheaper than you think with 'Explorer' tickets. 'Explorers' are 'go anywhere' one day tickets from £6 per adult, £3 per child, £4.20 per senior citizen or £11.50 for a family ticket. 'Busabouts' offer unlimited travel on seven consecutive days at bargain prices, please call for details. Look out for the Wilts & Dorset Out and About leaflets and use this guide to give you lots of bright ideas for planning great days out. For more information please telephone the Bus Station at Poole, 01202 673555 or Salisbury, 01722 336855. **Price B Check out page 10.**

HAMPSHIRE

Stagecoach South East, www.stagecoachbus.com 0845 121 0170. Exploring by bus is excellent value and avoids parking space dilemmas in major tourist areas. The Stagecoach Coastliner, route 700, is a frequent service between Southsea and Brighton providing links across the south, including Portsmouth Hard, for connections to the Isle of Wight. Available in adult, child and family versions, the one-day Goldrider tickets offer unlimited travel on all Stagecoach buses across the South East; the Triplelink range of tickets gets a family of five to Ryde Esplanade on the Isle of Wight for around £30. With six options to choose from, the Triplelink also saves money on the entrance to various attractions on the island, including the Isle of Wight Steam Railway and Osborne House. Stagecoach offers various combined entrance and travel tickets for a number of the best attractions along the south coast, including, Portsmouth Historic Dockyard and all tickets provide great savings on paying for the bus and entrance separately. **Check out page 6.**

ISLE OF WIGHT

Sandown, Southern Vectis, 01983 532373. Open-top bus service to Shanklin Esplanade, Easter-Sept. Schools **Price B.**

Yarmouth, Southern Vectis, 01983 532373. Open-top bus service to the Needles, Easter-Sept. Schools **Price B.**

HORSE-DRAWN TRIPS

SALISBURY AREA

Salisbury, Wessex Horse Omnibus, from the Guildhall, 07718 046814. Rides around the city and through the river run Easter-late Autumn, Mon-Sat, from 10.30am (weather permitting). Pre-booking advisable. Birthdays **Price B.**

TANK DRIVING

HAMPSHIRE

Winchester, Juniper Leisure, (must be pre-booked) 01794 367367. Mar-Oct.

TRAIN TRIPS

DORSET

Swanage, Swanage Railway, www.swanagerailway.co.uk 01929 425800, has recreated a six mile stretch of the Purbeck Line from Swanage to Norden via the historic village of Corfe Castle. At Norden, park and ride facilities are available, enabling you to leave your car and enjoy a steam ride through the beautiful Purbeck Hills to Corfe Castle and Swanage. Trains run every weekend throughout the year and daily, Apr-Oct. Popular Santa Specials run every weekend in Dec up to Christmas. Schools **Price C Check out page 12.**

HAMPSHIRE

Alresford, Mid-Hants Watercress Line, www.watercressline.co.uk 01962 733810, (Talking Timetable, 01962 734866). Enjoy a great day out and journey back in time on a genuine steam train. The Watercress Line runs for ten miles between Alresford and Alton and special events are organised throughout the year with children and families in mind, including a treat for Mothers Day, `War on the Line' where passengers can experience the 1940s, and the `Bus Rally'. Other exciting days out for children are `Day out with Thomas' events at Easter and in Aug, and magical `Santa Specials' in Dec. Open mid Jan–early Nov. Please telephone for details. Schools Birthdays Price C Check out below.

ISLE OF WIGHT

Havenstreet, Isle of Wight Steam Railway, near Ryde, www.iwsteamrailway.co.uk Talking Timetable: 01983 882204/884343. Calling at Smallbrook, Ashey, Havenstreet, Wootton. Open selected times Apr-Oct, and daily, Jun-Sept, 10.30am-3.30pm. Schools Price B.

Ryde, Dotto Land Train, Appley Pitch and Putt, 01983 402447, travels a circular route from the park into the town. Open daily, Easter-Oct, 10am-6pm (8pm Jun-Aug). Price A.

Sandown, Dotto Land Train, The Esplanade, 01983 402447, travels along the Esplanade. Open daily, Easter-Oct, 10am-6pm (8pm Jun-Aug). Price A.

Shanklin, Dotto Land Train, The Esplanade, 01983 402447, travels a circular route to Shanklin Old Village. Open daily, Easter-Oct, 10am-6pm (8pm Jun-Aug). Price A.

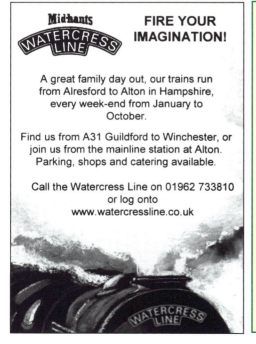

FIRE YOUR IMAGINATION!

A great family day out, our trains run from Alresford to Alton in Hampshire, every week-end from January to October.

Find us from A31 Guildford to Winchester, or join us from the mainline station at Alton. Parking, shops and catering available.

Call the Watercress Line on 01962 733810 or log onto www.watercressline.co.uk

Swanage Railway Co. Ltd.
Station House, Swanage,
Dorset. BH19 1HB
TEL: (01929) 425800

Travel on Dorset's Award Winning Steam Railway and enjoy unique views of historic *Corfe Castle.*

Park & Ride open all year round at Norden, just north of Corfe Castle and additional parking at Harmans Cross

Coach parking at Norden, also Wilts & Dorset service buses operate via Norden car park on train operating days.

Adventure & Fun

Quite a medley here, with a strong emphasis on fun and play, rides and thrills. This chapter includes theme parks, indoor play centres, other fun activities and themed venues such as laser game centres, water fun parks and maize mazes. You may even find some farm venues listed where the main attractions on offer diversify from animals into adventure play giving the best of both worlds!

DORSET

Bournemouth, Bournemouth International Centre Leisure Pool, Exeter Road, 01202 456580, has fun slides, waves and float sessions. **Open all year.**
Bournemouth Seafront, 01202 451781. An amusement arcade and small fairground rides number among the entertainments on offer. **Price P.**
Quasar, Glenfern Road, 01202 291717, for fun indoor laser gun games. **Open all year Price A.**
Sega Park, Westover Road, 01202 316396, for the latest in interactive electronic entertainment. Open Mon-Wed, 10am-10pm, Thurs-Sat, 9am-11pm, Sun, 10am-10pm. **Open all year Price P.**
Streetwise Safety Centre, Elliott Road, www.streetwise.org.uk www.homesafetygame.com 01202 591330. A life-size indoor village built to raise awareness of everyday safety. Fun, educational and 'Streetwise Saves Lives'. Open Mon-Fri, 9am-5pm, plus weekends and evenings by arrangement. Advance booking only. Schools Birthdays **Open all year Price B.**

Christchurch, Alice in Wonderland Family Park, opposite Bournemouth Airport, www.aliceinwonderlandpark.co.uk 01202 483444. Meet Alice and friends amidst themed attractions, including the Runaway Train Rollercoaster, Flying Elephants, YoYo Ride and Giant Astroslide. Open daily, Easter-mid Sept, 10am-last entry 4pm, then Sat-Sun only until Oct half-term, when open all week. Schools Birthdays **Price C.**
Serendipity Sam's, Reid Street, www.serendipitysams.co.uk 0845 450 7200. An indoor play venue for children up to age 11 to enjoy brightly coloured slides, ball pools and rope swings in a safe and supervised environment. Socks must be worn. Open daily, phone for opening times. Birthdays **Open all year Price A.**
Stewarts Gardenlands, 01425 272244. Discover this exciting maize maze between Jul and Sept. Phone for details.

Gillingham, Funny Farm, 01747 821825. Climb up high, gaze in mirrors and lose yourself in ball pools at this indoor and outdoor adventure play area for under 10s. Open daily, 10am-6.30pm. Birthdays **Open all year Price A.**

Poole, Gus Gorilla's Jungle Playground, Poole Park, 01202 717197. Swing from Tarzan ropes and brave the aerial walkways in this indoor adventure fun park. Height restrictions. Hourly rate. Open daily, 10am-6pm. Birthdays **Open all year Price A.**
Splashdown, Tower Park, 01202 716123. Make a big splash on this water slide. Open Mon-Fri, 2-9pm, Sat-Sun, 10am-7pm. Call for school hols openings. **Price C.**

Swanage, The Bandstand. There is an amusement park for small children and crazy golf. **Price P.**

Warmwell, Warmwell Leisure Resort, 01305 852911. Make waves in the pool and enjoy soft play at this fun-park resort. Birthdays.

Weymouth, Deep Sea Adventure and Sharky's Play and Party Warehouse, Custom House Quay, 0871 222 5760. Enjoy Sharky's indoor adventure playground or explore two floors of nautical history, featuring the Titanic and local shipwrecks and learn about the history of diving. You can now paint your own pottery at First 4 Art. Open daily, 9.30am-6pm. Schools Birthdays **Open all year Price B.**

It's the big, bright, brilliant, buzzing place for kidz who want to be kidz & adults who want to let them! It's fizzical fun for everyone, so come & have a go!
Open 10am to 7pm, every day.

**PLAY ZONE, Unit A4
Oak Park Industrial Estate, North Harbour Rd,
PORTSMOUTH**

023 92 37 99 99

www.theplayzone.co.uk
Children must be supervised by an adult at all times.
PLAYZONE reserve the right to refuse entry.

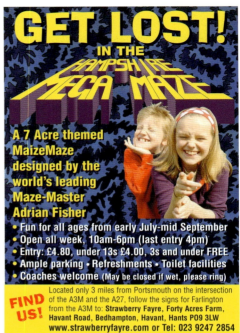

GET LOST!
IN THE HAMPSHIRE MECA MAZE

A 7 Acre themed MaizeMaze designed by the world's leading Maze-Master Adrian Fisher

- Fun for all ages from early July-mid September
- Open all week, 10am-6pm (last entry 4pm)
- Entry: £4.80, under 13s £4.00, 3s and under FREE
- Ample parking • Refreshments • Toilet facilities
- Coaches welcome (May be closed if wet, please ring)

FIND US! Located only 3 miles from Portsmouth on the intersection of the A3M and the A27, follow the signs for Farlington from the A3M to: **Strawberry Fayre, Forty Acres Farm, Havant Road, Bedhampton, Havant, Hants PO9 3LW**
www.strawberryfayre.com or Tel: 023 9247 2854

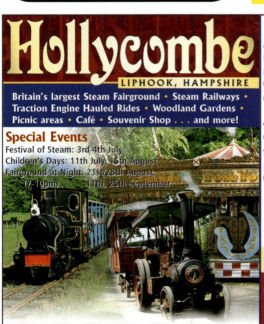

Hollycombe
LIPHOOK, HAMPSHIRE

Britain's largest Steam Fairground • Steam Railways •
Traction Engine Hauled Rides • Woodland Gardens •
Picnic areas • Café • Souvenir Shop . . . and more!

Special Events
Festival of Steam: 3rd-4th July
Children's Days: 11th July, 15th August
Fairground at Night: 21st/28th August,
(7-10pm)   11th, 25th September

Open days in 2004

4th April to 10th October: Sundays and Bank Holidays, including all Easter weekend.

Daily between 1st and 30th August
(Fairground and one railway operate on weekdays)

Open 12 noon to 5pm, rides from 1pm.

Admission: Adults: £8.50,

Children (3-15) & OAPs: £7.00, **Saver Ticket: £28.00**

Weekday prices: (Mon-Sat 2nd-28th August)
£1 less per person
(Saver Tickets admit up to 4 people: no more than 2 adults)

Pre-booked Party Rates on application

All rides are included in the admission price.
Dogs are only allowed in the car park. All attractions subject to availability.

www.hollycombe.co.uk
Tel: **01428 724900**

Lodmoor Country Park, Leisureranch, 01305 761420. Fun for all the family with go-karts, bumper boats and the cresta run. Also on offer are pitch and putt, model world and a miniature railway. Enjoy the RSPB Nature Reserve or visit the Sea Life Centre. Check out `Farms'. Nature Reserve open all year, Amusement Park, Easter-Oct, daily, 10am-6pm. **Schools Birthdays Price P.**

Weymouth(near), Beachside Leisure Centre, Bowleaze Cove. Fairground fun with dodgems, a helter skelter and an amusement arcade. There are also mini racing cars and motor bikes. Open Apr-Oct. **Price P.**

Rodden Farmhouse, Rodden, 01305 871281. Come and discover the Great Dorset Maize Maze between Jul and Sept. Phone for details.

Adventure & Fun

HAMPSHIRE

Alton, Treehouse, Draymans Way, 01420 549649. Go crazy in the indoor and outdoor adventure playgrounds. Open Mon-Sat, 10am-6pm, Sun, 10am-4pm. **Price A.**

Andover, Archie's World, Andover Leisure Centre, 01264 347100. Ball pools, slides and nets make for indoor play fun. Open daily, 9am-6pm. **Birthdays Open all year Price A.**

Jungle Jungle, Unit 3A West Way, 01264 336360. Enjoy the challenges of the Amazon trail in this indoor adventure land. Under 11s only. Open daily, 9.30am-5.30pm. Hourly rate. **Birthdays Open all year Price A.**

Basingstoke, Aquadrome, Basingstoke Leisure Park, 01256 472343. Three slides, river rapid and lagoon area for exciting watery fun. Open Mon-Fri, 4-8pm, Sat-Sun, 10am-7pm; school hols, Mon-Fri, 10am-8pm, Sat-Sun, 10am-7pm. **Birthdays Open all year Price B.**

Fun House, Whitney Road, 01256 471066. Under 12s can enjoy three levels of fun with slides, ropes, nets, ball pools and more. Open daily, Mon-Fri, 10am-6pm, Sat, 10am-7.30pm, Sun, 10am-5pm. **Birthdays Open all year Price A.**

Bedhampton, Hampshire Mega Maze, 40 Acre Farm, www.strawberryfayre.com 023 9247 2854. This seven-acre growing conundrum offers an entertaining half day out for families who enjoy fresh air, exercise and fun. Explore over two and a half miles of pathways with three bridges in a themed maize maze. If you get lost, put up a flag and a maze helper will rescue you! There are novel games for you to try, puzzles to solve and a great Fun Zone with refreshments. Open daily during the Summer holidays (subject to weather conditions) 10am-6pm, last entry 4.30pm. **Price B Check out page 14.**

Chandlers Ford, Space Ace, Renown Close, 023 8025 5777. An action-packed indoor adventure play centre. Giant slides, ball pools and rope nets beckon. Under 5s can try the Lunar Walk in a special area. Max height 145cm. Hourly rate per child. Open daily, Mon-Fri, 10am-7pm, Sat-Sun, 10am-8pm. **Birthdays Open all year Price A.**

Dibden, Pirates Paradise, Applemore Recreation Centre, 023 8084 4288. Visit the two-deck pirate ship indoor play area with specially designed toddlers' area. Max height 147cm. Open Mon, Tues, Thurs, 9.30am-6pm, Wed and Fri, 9.30am-7pm, Sat, 9am-8pm, Sun, 9am-6pm. **Birthdays Open all year Price A.**

Fareham, Fun City, 32 Standard Way, 01329 511055. Let off steam in this soft play zone with ball pits, nets and ropes. Max height 147cm. Open daily, Mon-Fri, 10am-6pm, Sat-Sun, 9am-6pm. **Birthdays Open all year Price A.**

Farnborough, Fizzy Kids, North Camp, 01252 669977. Let off steam at this indoor play centre for up to 11 year olds. **Birthdays Open all year Price A.**

Run-About, Armstrong Way, www.run-about.co.uk 01252 370721. Two-level play area with slides, ball pits and tunnels for under 10s. Height limit 140cm. Open Mon-Fri, 9.30am-6pm, Sat-Sun, 10am-6pm. **Birthdays Open all year Price A.**

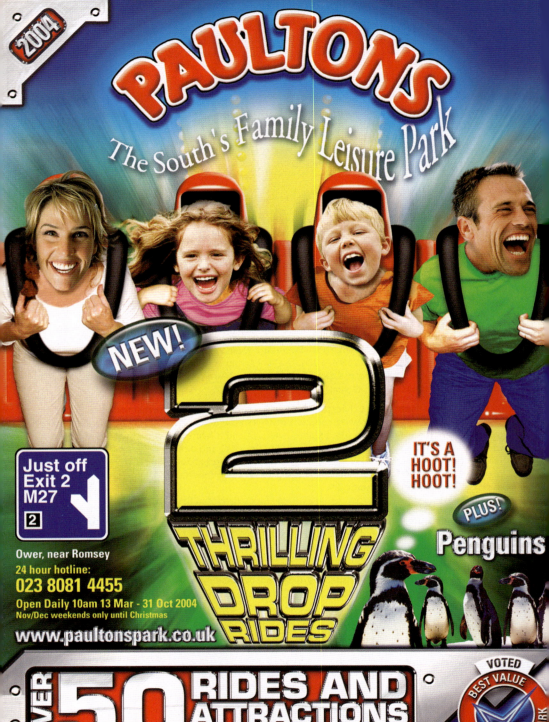

Star Quest and Tumble Junction, Farnborough Recreation Centre, Westmead, 01252 370411. Climb and slide into ball pools at this indoor centre. **Birthdays Open all year Price A.**
Wizzy World Adventure Play, Invincible Road, www.wizzy-world.com 0845 226 2329, has play frames and slides. Open daily, 9.30am-6.30pm. **Birthdays Open all year Price A.**

Hayling Island, Funlands Amusement Park, Seafront, 023 9246 2820, includes a log ride and an indoor amusement complex. Call for opening times. **Price P.**

Hedge End, Krazy Kingdom, 01489 790795. A three-tier play structure with slides, ball pit and toddler area. Open daily, 9am-6pm. **Birthdays Open all year Price A.**

Liphook, Hollycombe Steam Collection, www.hollycombe.co.uk 01428 724900, is one of the world's largest working steam fairgrounds. The wide variety of Edwardian steam-powered attractions provides family entertainment in a rural setting, giving an insight into different aspects of Britain's heritage. Working steam-driven exhibits include a spectacular galloper's roundabout, the ever-popular Haunted House, three railways, traction engines and rare swingboats once common in fairgrounds. Fairground organs and sidestalls help create the cheerful atmosphere. Farm animals such as shire horses are certain to appeal to younger children. Many lovely walks are available, as are light refreshments, together with an excellent picnic area. The inclusive entrance fee entitles you to an unlimited number of rides. Open all Easter weekend, Suns and Bank Hols, 4th Apr-10th Oct (daily, 1st-30th Aug), 12noon-5pm. Rides from 1pm. **Schools Price C Check out page 14.**

Portsmouth, Playzone, Unit A4, Oak Park Industrial Estate, North Harbour Road, www.the-playzone.co.uk 023 9237 9999. Whatever the weather, children can enjoy the latest play equipment in this challenging and exciting indoor adventure play area of over 603 sqm. They can test their skills by crawling and squeezing through webs and rollers, drop down daredevil slides or find their way through tubes, mazes and ball pools. Laser Zone, a laser shootout game, will tempt all ages (evenings only). Relax in the relative calm of the café where a full range of hot and cold food is available. Open daily, 10am-7pm, main sessions are for 1-12 year olds; 13+ sessions every Wed, 7.30-9.30pm. **Schools Birthdays Open all year Price A Check out page 14.**

Ringwood(near), Matchams Leisure Park, Hurn Road, www.ringwoodraceway.com 01425 473305. Fun Karts suitable for children and adults. Open May Bank Hol-Sept, 10am-4pm. **Birthdays Price P.**

Romsey, The Rapids, Romsey Leisure Centre www.valleyleisure.com 01794 830333. Special features make use of the latest technology and include the rapids, a storm shower, warm spa pools and underwater 'bubble' seats and flume ride. Open Mon-Fri, 10am-9pm, Sat, 10am-7pm, Sun, 10am-8pm. **Birthdays Open all year Price B.**
Serendipity Sam's, Unit 3 Romsey Industrial Estate, Greatbridge Road, www.serendipitysams.co.uk 0845 450 7200. A large fun indoor play venue for children up to age 11 to enjoy brightly coloured slides, ball pools and rope swings. Socks must be worn. Open daily, phone for times. **Birthdays Open all year Price A.**

Romsey(near), Paultons Park, Ower, Jn2 off M27, www.paultonspark.co.uk Booking office: 023 8081 4442, 24hr hotline: 023 8081 4455. Set within 140 acres of beautiful parkland with over 50 different attractions and rides, an action-packed day out is guaranteed. New for 2004 is the Jumping Bean, a thrilling vertical drop ride, which rises to 12m before plummeting back down to earth when least expected and also Jumping Jack, a mini drop ride giving younger children and the less intrepid the chance to experience the excitement of free falling. Rides and entertainments include the Wave Runner, Flying Frog rollercoaster, Pirate Ship, Stinger Rollercoaster, Raging River Ride log flume, Teacup Ride, Dragon Ride and the Astroglide. Younger children will love Kids Kingdom, Land of the Dinosaurs, Seal Falls and Digger Rides, Whirlycopter, Tiny Tots Town, the Wonderful World of Wind in the Willows and the Magic Forest, where nursery rhymes come to life at the touch of a button. Also enjoy the Romany Experience and Village Life Museums, Hedge

Maze and bird gardens with over 250 species. The latest addition to Paultons extensive bird collection are Humboldt penguins. Daily keeper talks and feeding sessions give a unique insight into these fascinating and humorous birds. There is a self-service restaurant, tearooms, take-away kiosks and picnic areas. Some rides have height restrictions. Open daily, mid Mar-end Oct, 10am-6.30pm, earlier in Winter, Nov-Dec, weekends only until Christmas. Also Santa's Christmas Wonderland where visits must be pre-booked. The Family Supersaver entry ticket offers great value and children under 1m are free. Schools Birthdays Price E Check out page 16.

Shirley, **Adventure Zone,** Marlborough Road, 023 8039 3350. Have fun on an array of padded play equipment including monster slides, wobbly bridge rollers and ball pools. Open Mon-Sat, 10am-6pm, Sun, 11am-4pm. Hourly rate. Birthdays Open all year.

Southampton, **Children's Pleasure Park,** Sports Centre, Bassett, 023 8043 1710, has a slide, swings and mini rides, and a miniature train runs. Open daily, Easter-Oct, 10.30am-6pm (weather permitting). Price P.
Laser Quest, Aukland Road, Millbrook, 023 8051 1511. Laser game fun. Open Mon-Fri, 12noon-10.30pm, Sat-Sun, 10am-10.30pm. Birthdays Open all year Price A.
Ollies Fun Centre, Royal Crescent Road, 023 8023 6123. Indoor fun with exciting adventure play facilities. Open Mon-Fri, 9am-6pm, Sat-Sun, 10am-6pm. Birthdays Open all year Price A.
The Quays, West Quay, 023 8072 0900. A swimming and diving complex. Phone for opening times and prices. Birthdays Open all year.
Sega Park, Bargate Shopping Centre, 023 8022 5067. State-of-the-art electronic games and simulators. Open daily, Mon-Sat, 9am-7pm, Sun, 10.30am-6pm. Birthdays Open all year Price P.

Southsea, **Clarence Pier Amusement Park,** Clarence Pier, www.clarencepier.co.uk 023 9282 0132, has lots of exciting fairground rides which include dodgems and a roller coaster. There are video games, simulators and an indoor amusement complex. Open daily, Easter-Sept. Price P.
Krazy Kaves, Dickinson Road, 023 9275 0077. Soft play fun on three levels for under 12s. Open daily, 9.30am-8pm. Birthdays Open all year Price A.
Pirate Pete's, Clarence Pier, 023 9286 4789. Soft play equipment and ball-pool fun. Hourly rate. Open daily, 9am-6pm. Birthdays Open all year.
The Pyramids Centre, Clarence Esplanade, 023 9279 9977. Make a splash and have fun with flumes and waves at this water fun park. Phone for opening times. Open all year Price B.
South Parade Pier, 023 9273 2283. Traditional amusements. Open daily, 10am-10pm. Open all year.
Southsea Common Skate Park, 023 9282 5005. Practise your routines on these purpose-designed ramps, bowls, rink and new jump box. Bring your own skates, padding and safety helmet. Open daily, times vary. Open all year Price A.

Whitchurch, **Serendipity Sam's,** 52 Evengar Road, www.serendipitysams.co.uk 0845 450 7200. An indoor play venue for children up to age 11 to enjoy brightly coloured slides, ball pools and rope swings in a safe and supervised environment. Socks must be worn. Open daily, phone for opening times. Birthdays Open all year Price A.

Winchester, **Ocean Adventure,** River Park Leisure Centre, Gordon Road, 01962 848700. Nets, slides and ball pools are to be found at this indoor play centre. Open daily, 10am-12.30pm, Mon-Thurs, 2-5pm. Call for school hols openings. Birthdays Open all year Price A.

SALISBURY AREA

Ansty, **Ansty PYO and Farm Shop,** 01747 829072, has a maize maze in Summer and the Pumpkin Olympics during Autumn half-term. Birthdays.

Salisbury, Outburst (includes Clown About, Strikers and Laser A), Unit 5, Milford Trading Estate, Blakey Road, www.outburstsalisbury.com 01722 413121. With an exciting two-level playstructure, laser tag and bowling, there is something for all the family. Open daily, times vary. **Birthdays Open all year Price P.**

ISLE OF WIGHT

Alum Bay, The Needles Park, www.theneedles.co.uk 01983 752401. Crazy golf, motion simulator, glass studio, sand shop and sweet manufactory. Take a chairlift ride over the multi-coloured cliffs towards the Needles (closed during Winter). Open daily, Easter-Oct, 10am-5pm, Nov-Easter, 10am-4pm. **Schools Birthdays Open all year Price P.**

Downend, Robin Hill, near Arreton, www.robin-hill.com 01983 527352. 'Time Machine' motion platform cinema and 400m Toboggan Run. Max height 110cm. Open 22nd Mar-30th Oct, 10am-5pm. **Schools Birthdays Price B.**

Newport, Headhunters Laser Combat, 62 Fairlee Road, 01983 520061. Ring to book a laser session. **Price A.**
Xtreme Play, Drill Hall Road, 01983 533737. Slides and ropeways provide soft play fun. Open daily, 10am-6pm. **Price A.**

Ryde, Peter Pan Playground, Ryde Seafront. An amusement park with numerous rides and carousel. Open Easter-Sept, 10am-6pm (later in high season). **Price P.**

Sandown, Magic Island, Sandown Pier, 01983 401754. Explore tunnels and slides at this soft play centre. Open Mon-Fri, 12noon-6pm term time, 10am-6pm during school hols, Sat-Sun, 10am-6pm. **Birthdays Open all year Price A.**
Sandown Rides, Fort Street, 01983 406600. Family fun with a giant slide, splash bumper boats and go-karts. Height restrictions apply. Open Easter-Oct, 10am-6pm (10am-10pm in high season). **Schools Price P.**

Shanklin, Jungle Jim's Adventure Play, Summer Arcade, Esplanade, 01983 867557. A soft play area with tube slides, ball pools, snake slide, family ten-pin bowling and crazy golf. Max height 150cm. Open daily, 9.30am-6.30pm. **Schools Birthdays Open all year Price A.**

Ventnor(near), Blackgang Chine, Chale, www.blackgangchine.com 01983 730330 or 24hr Helpline: 01983 730052. Take a ride on Water Force, explore Smugglers Cave, Land full of Dinosaurs and more. Open 22nd Mar-31st Oct, 10am-5pm, (10am-10pm in Summer hols). **Schools Birthdays Price C.**

TRAVEL GAMES

What can you see from the car window?
If there are 2 or more of you, who can see the following things first? Keep score!

Caravan	Zebra crossing	Traffic lights
Dog	Black and white cows	Bridge
Motorway sign	Car transporter	Milk float
Tunnel	Sheep	Stretch limousine
Level crossing	Red letter box	Telephone box

Adventure & Fun

Visiting Relations? Going On Holiday? Gift For A Friend?

Mail Order Price £4.00 each inc p&p

Now available for every county in England
A complete guide to places of interest and things to do for children aged 3 to 16 yrs

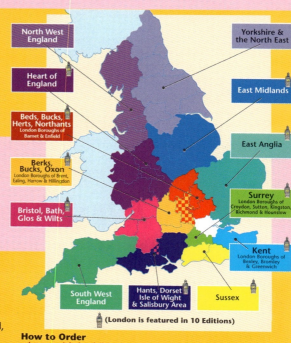

- **Beds, Bucks, Herts, Northants**
  & London Boroughs of Barnet & Enfield
- **Berks, Bucks & Oxon**
  & London Boroughs of Brent, Ealing, Harrow & Hillingdon
- **Bristol, Bath, Glos & Wilts**
  (Cotswolds & Forest of Dean)
- **East Anglia**
  (Cambs, Essex, Norfolk & Suffolk)
- **East Midlands**
  (Derby, Leics, Lincs, Notts & Rutland)
- **Hants, Dorset,**
  Isle of Wight & Salisbury Area
- **Heart of England**
  (Hereford, Shrops, Staffs, Warwicks, Worcs, W.Midlands)
- **Kent**
  & London Boroughs of Bexley, Bromley & Greenwich
- **North West**
  (Cheshire, Cumbria, Lancashire, Manchester, Merseyside)
- **South West**
  (Devon, Cornwall & Somerset)
- **Surrey**
  & London Boroughs of Croydon, Sutton, Kingston, Richmond & Hounslow
- **Sussex**
- **Yorkshire & the North East**
  (Durham, Humberside, Northumberland, Teeside, Tyne & Wear)

(London is featured in 10 Editions)

How to Order
- On Line: www.letsgowiththechildren.co.uk
- By Phone: 01425 279001 with your credit card details
- By Post: Send order with your name, address & email and a cheque made payable to Cube Publications to:

Cube Publications Mail Order
290 Lymington Rd, Highcliffe, Christchurch, Dorset BH23 5ET
email: enquiries@cubepublications.co.uk

History, Art & Science

Step back in time and learn about the past, both historical and military. Explore the world of art and design or discover the mysteries of science and technology. The places listed here have admission charges, but there are many wonderful museums and places of interest which are free to visit. Check out 'Free Places' as well, so you don't miss anything.

For opening times & prices at English Heritage sites please call 0870 333 1181 or check out www.english-heritage.org.uk

DORSET

Blandford Camp, The Royal Signals Museum, www.royalsignals.army.org.uk/museum 01258 482248, tells the story of military communications from the Crimean War to the present day. Displays about the science and technology of communications are combined with interactive exhibitions. Learn about Enigma and send Morse code. New for 2004 'Dorset and D-Day' exhibition. Open Mon-Fri, 10am-5pm, Sat-Sun, 10am-4am. Nov-mid Feb, closed Sat-Sun. Schools Open all year Price B.

Blandford Forum, Cavalcade of Costume, Lime Tree House, 01258 453006. Over 250 years of costume history in this interesting museum where each garment has a story attached to it. Open Thurs-Mon, Easter-Sept, 11am-4.30pm, Oct-Easter, 11am-3.30pm. Closed Dec-Feb. Schools Price A.

Bovington, The Tank Museum, www.tankmuseum.co.uk 01929 405096, contains the world's finest international collection of armoured fighting vehicles. New Home Front exhibition. During the school Summer hols, Tanks in Action displays demonstrate their awesome firepower. Restaurant, picnic area and outdoor play area. Open daily, 10am-5pm. Schools Open all year Price C.

Bradford Peverell, New Barn Field Centre, near Dorchester, www.newbarn.co.uk 01305 268865. Discover a reconstructed Iron-Age homestead and find out about our prehistoric ancestors. Follow the nature trail or experience some pottery. Open daily, Aug, 10am-5pm. Schools at other times by arrangement. Schools Price A.

Christchurch, Bournemouth Aviation Museum, Hangar 600, Bournemouth International Airport, www.aviation-museum.co.uk 01202 580858. An operational base where the public can view ex-military vintage jet aircraft such as the Hunter, Vampire, BAC1-11 and Mig 17. Recent additions include a Vulcan cockpit and a Hunter aircraft cockpit open to the public. Vickers Vanguard Simulator. Open daily, Apr-Sept, 10am-5pm, Oct-Mar, 10am-4pm. Schools Open all year Price B.

Highcliffe Castle, 01425 278807. Built between 1830 and 1835 during William IV's reign, the Grade I listed and partially restored castle has medieval French masonry incorporated in its structure and a French 16th-century stained glass window in the Great Hall. Open daily, 1st Apr-23rd Dec, 11am-4.30pm (3.30pm in Winter). Schools Price A.

Museum of Electricity, Bargates, 01202 480467. Hands-on working models and early domestic items feature here. A shocking time is guaranteed! Open Mon-Thurs, (Fri during school hols), Easter-Sept, 12noon-4.30pm. Schools Price A.

Red House Museum and Gardens, Quay Road, 01202 482860, has a costume gallery, 1930s room, archaeology gallery and excellent natural history displays. Open Tues-Sat and Bank Hol Mons, 10am-5pm, Sun, 2-5pm. Free admission to residents of Hants and Dorset. Schools Open all year Price A.

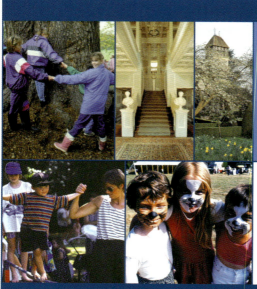

History, Art & Science

Corfe Castle, **Corfe Castle,** NT, 01929 481294. Imagine the Civil War sieges as you climb the steep hill to the impressive castle ruins. Living History weekends are planned throughout the year, and there is a visitor display at Castle View car park. Tearoom and visitor centre. Open daily, Mar, 10am-5pm, Apr-Oct, 10am-6pm, Nov-Feb, 10am-4pm. Schools Open all year Price B.

Dorchester, **The Dinosaur Museum,** Icen Way, www.world-heritage.org.uk 01305 269880, successfully combines actual fossils, skeletons and life-size dinosaur reconstructions with audio-visual, interactive and computer displays. Open daily, Apr-Oct, 9am-5.30pm, Nov-Mar, 9.30am-4.30pm. Schools Open all year Price B.
Dorset County Museum, High West Street, www.dorsetcountymuseum.org.uk 01305 262735, contains dinosaur footprints, a reconstruction of Thomas Hardy's study and archaeological items from nearby Maiden Castle. Open Mon-Sat, May-Oct Sun also, 10am-5pm. Schools Open all year Price A.
The Keep Military Museum, Bridport Road, www.keepmilitarymuseum.org.uk 01305 264066, covers the history of the infantry, cavalry and artillery of the counties of Devon and Dorset, from 1685 to the present day. Open Apr-Sept, Mon-Sat, Oct-Mar, Tues-Sat, 9.30am-5pm, Jul-Aug, Sun also, 10am-4pm. Schools Open all year Price A.
Teddy Bear House, Antelope Walk, www.teddybearmuseum.co.uk 01305 263200. See human-size bears relaxing at home in this Dorset teddy museum. Open daily, 9.30am-5pm. Winter Sun opening times, 10am-4.30pm. Schools Open all year Price A.
Tutankhamun Exhibition, High West Street, 01305 269571. Walk through the reconstructed chambers with audio explanations of its discovery and the treasures found. Open daily, Easter-Oct, 9.30am-5.30pm, Nov-Easter, Mon-Fri, 9.30am-5pm, Sat, 10am-5pm, Sun, 10am-4.30pm. Schools Open all year Price B.

East Lulworth, **Lulworth Castle,** www.lulworth.com 01929 400352. Climb the castle tower and enjoy the parkland setting here. There is an Animal Farm open Easter-Oct. Castle open Sun-Fri, Easter-Oct, 10.30am-6pm, Nov-Easter, 10.30am-4pm. Schools Open all year Price B.

Isle of Portland, **Portland Castle,** EH, 01305 820539. Discover one of Henry VIII's finest coastal fortresses, perfectly preserved in a waterfront location overlooking Portland harbour. Explore the Tudor kitchen and gun platform, see ghostly sculpted figures from the past and enjoy superb battlement views. Children's activity room and educational groups free if pre-booked. Open daily, Apr-Oct, 10am-6pm (5pm Oct), Nov-Mar, Fri-Sun, 10am-4pm. Schools Open all year Price B.

Lyme Regis, **Dinosaurland,** Coombe Street, www.dinosaurland.co.uk 01297 443541. An interesting museum with dioramas on the Jurassic Age. Guided fossil beach walks are available and a fossil clinic, where your find can be identified, and advice given on cleaning and preserving. Open daily, 10am-5pm (6pm Jul-Aug). Schools Open all year Price B.

Sherborne, **Sherborne Castle,** www.sherbornecastle.com 01935 813182, houses furniture, paintings and porcelain of interest to older children. Beautiful landscaped grounds provide lakeside walks and parkland picnic spaces. Open Apr-Oct, Tues-Thurs, Sat-Sun, Bank Hol Mons. Castle, shop and tearoom, 11am-4.30pm (Sat, Castle 2.30-4.30pm). Up to 4 children free with 1 paying adult. (Joint ticketing with Sherborne Old Castle.) Schools Price B.
Sherborne Old Castle, EH, off B3145, 01935 812730. The 12th-century castle ruins are a testament to the 16 days Cromwell took to capture it during the Civil War. Magnificent views, picnic area. Educational groups free if pre-booked. Open daily, Apr-Oct, 10am-6pm (5pm Oct). Schools Price A.

Weymouth, **Discovery,** Brewers Quay, www.discoverdiscovery.co.uk 01305 789007, offers hands-on science fun for all ages. With 60 interactive exhibits, features include special mirror effects, an intelligent robotic arm and marble run. Open daily, 10am-5.30pm, school Summer hols, 10am-9pm. Phone for Winter opening times. Schools Birthdays Open all year Price B.

Nothe Fort, 01305 766626. Climb the ramparts of this Victorian fort and see displays of military life. Follow the trail of toy mice hidden around the maze of tunnels. Open daily, May-Sept, 10.30am-5.30pm. Groups by arrangement at other times. (Up to 4 accompanied children under 16 free.) Schools Price A.

The Timewalk, Brewers Quay, 01305 777622. An interactive family gallery that tells the town's story through the eyes of the brewery cat, Ms Paws, and her ancestors. Open daily, 10am-last admission 4.30pm, Summer hols, 10am-9pm. Closed last two weeks Jan. Schools Open all year Price B.

Wimborne, Priest's House Museum and Garden, High Street, 01202 882533. There are reconstructions of an ironmonger's, a Victorian kitchen, an archaeology gallery and a Costume and Textile gallery. Open Apr-Oct, Mon-Sat, 10am-4.30pm. Schools Price A.

Wimborne Minster Model Town, www.wimborne-modeltown.com 01202 881924. Charming scale model of Wimborne in the 1950s. A quiz trail, model railway, Wendy House play area and tearooms make a pleasant visit. Open daily, 26th Mar-3rd Oct, 10am-5pm. Phone for details of special events. Schools Price A.

Wimborne(near), Kingston Lacy House and Park, NT, on the B3082, 01202 883402. Set in beautiful landscaped gardens, the 17th-century house contains a fine European art collection. House open 20th Mar-31st Oct, Wed-Sun, 11am-4pm, grounds daily, 10.30am-6pm. Phone for Winter opening times of grounds. Schools Price A/B.

HAMPSHIRE

Aldershot, Airborne Forces Museum, Browning Barracks, 01252 349619, has an aeroplane and guns on display outside. Inside, the story of Britain's Airborne Forces is well depicted. Open daily, 10am-4pm. Schools Open all year Price A.

Aldershot Military Museum, Queens Avenue, 01252 314598, depicts military and civilian life over 150 years and includes local history, World War II, and early aviation galleries. Open daily, 10am-5pm. Schools Open all year Price A.

Basing, Basing House, 01256 467294, is now only ruins but there is an exhibition here of its long history. A 17th-century formal garden has been recreated and there are many pleasant places to walk and enjoy a picnic. Phone for details of special events. Open Apr-Sept, Wed-Sun, 2-6pm and Bank Hols. Schools Price A.

Basingstoke, Milestones, Leisure Park, Churchill Way West, www.milestones-museum.com 01256 477766, tells the story of everyday life at home and at work in the Victorian period and in the 1930s. Thousands of objects collected from all over Hampshire are displayed in authentic, recreated streets complete with shops, houses and factories. Scenes are brought to life by costumed staff – hear the tales of life as a factory worker, or play traditional games popular with Victorian school children. See how the washing was done or call into Abrahams the confectioners and 'purchase' sweets with a wartime ration card. Gift shop and café. Open Tues-Fri, 10am-5pm, Sat-Sun, 11am-5pm and Bank Hol Mons, 10am-5pm. Schools Open all year Price B Check out page 22.

Beaulieu, The National Motor Museum, Palace House and Abbey Ruins, www.beaulieu.co.uk 01590 612391. Look out for the Motor Sports Gallery housing Formula One cars and the James Bond boat exhibition. Take a Veteran Bus or Car Ride through the Palace grounds or board the Monorail. Enjoy the Palace House and the Abbey. School hols activities and guided tours. Open daily, 10am-6pm (5pm Winter). Schools Open all year Price D.

Bishops Waltham, Bishops Waltham Palace, EH, 01489 892460. The remains of the medieval residence of the Bishops of Winchester stand in beautiful grounds, ideal for picnics. Schools must pre-book. Phone for opening details and prices. Schools.

Bucklers Hard, **The Maritime Museum,** 01590 616203, relates the story of the village's ship building history with recreated scenes of 18th-century life. Enjoy a river cruise Apr-Oct (check out `Trips') or beautiful riverside walks. Open daily, Easter-Oct, 10am-6pm, Nov-Easter, 11am-4.30pm. Schools Open all year Price B.

Bursledon, **Bursledon Windmill,** near Southampton, 023 8040 4999. Hampshire's only working windmill – call in whenever the sails are turning! A traditional timber-framed barn and granary have been reconstructed on the site, together with a farm pond. Open May-Sept, Sat-Sun, 10am-4pm, Oct-Apr, Sun, 10am-4pm. Schools Open all year Price A.

Calshot, **Calshot Castle,** EH, 023 8089 2023. Built by Henry VIII to command the sea passage to Southampton, the fort has provided a base for both the RN and RAF, with a barrack room restored to its pre-World War I artillery garrison appearance. Phone for opening details and prices. Schools.

Chawton, **Jane Austen's House,** 01420 83262, is where the author wrote or revised her six great novels. Open daily, Mar-Nov, 11am-4.30pm, Dec-Feb, Sat-Sun only. Schools Open all year Price A.

Fordingbridge(near), **Breamore House and Countryside Museum,** on A338, 01725 512468. An Elizabethan manor and museum portraying village life. Adventure playground and brick maze. Open 4th Apr-end Sept. In Apr, Tues and Sun, 1-5.30pm, (house opens at 2pm), May-Jul, Sept, Tues-Thurs, Sat-Sun, and daily in Aug and Bank Hols. Schools Price B.

Gosport, **EXPLOSION!** Priddy's Hard, www.explosion.org.uk 023 9250 5600. Learn about naval firepower, from gunpowder to the Exocet, and life as a female munitions worker during World War II. New for 2004 'The Blunt End – The Build-Up to D-Day'. Open daily, Apr-Oct and school hols, 10am-5.30pm; Nov-Mar, Thurs, Sat, Sun and Bank Hols, 10am-4.30pm. Schools Open all year Price B.
Fort Brockhurst, EH, 023 9258 1059. Enter the circular keep of this Victorian fort, cross the parade grounds and wander into the mess and washrooms. Phone for opening details and prices. Schools.
Royal Navy Submarine Museum, www.rnsubmus.co.uk 023 9252 9217, features the UK's major walk-on submarine, HMS Alliance. Imagine what it must be like to voyage aboard so deep under the sea. Open daily, Apr-Oct, 10am-5.30pm, Nov-Mar, 10am-4.30pm. Schools Open all year Price B.

Hurst Spit, **Hurst Castle,** EH, 01590 642344. Low and menacing on its shingle spit, Hurst Castle is one of the most sophisticated fortresses built by Henry VIII to defend the narrow entrance to the Solent. There are four exhibitions in the castle and two 38-ton guns from the fort's armaments. Phone for opening details and prices. Schools.

Lymington, **St Barbe Museum and Art Gallery,** New Street, 01590 676969. Two galleries of changing art and craft exhibitions and museum displays of local history and culture. Open Mon-Sat, 10am-4pm. Schools Open all year Price A.

Lyndhurst, **New Forest Museum and Visitor Centre,** main car park, 023 8028 3914. Newly refurbished, discover the traditions, wildlife and characters of the New Forest. Schools Open all year Price A.

Middle Wallop, **Museum of Army Flying and Explorers' World,** www.flying-museum.org.uk 01980 674421, celebrates over 100 years of army aviation and is home to one of the country's finest historical collections of military balloons, kites, gliders, aircraft and helicopters. Explorers' World, the Interactive Science and Education Centre, features an imaginative range of hands-on activities and experiments. Open daily, 10am-4.30pm. Schools Open all year Price B.

Mottisfont, **Mottisfont Abbey,** NT, near Romsey, 01794 340757. The River Test flows through the gardens of this 12th century Augustinian priory where walled gardens contain the National Collection of old-fashioned roses. See Whistler's trompe-l'oeil fantasy-style drawing room. Open 6th-21st Mar, Sat-Sun, 11am-4pm; 22nd Mar-31st Oct, 11am-6pm, Sat-Wed/daily, Abbey and gardens. Phone for precise opening details. Schools Price B **Check out 22.**

Netley, **Royal Victoria Country Park,** 023 8045 5157. Netley Chapel houses an exhibition on the Royal Victoria Military Hospital. Climb the 43m tower for a spectacular view of Southampton Water. Educational activities available from park office. Open daily, Apr-Oct, 12noon-4.30pm. Sun, 11am-4.30pm. Phone for Winter opening. Schools Price A.

Newbury, **Highclere Castle,** www.highclerecastle.co.uk 01635 253210, is an impressive early 19th-century castle in extensive park and gardens, the home of the Earls of Carnarvon. The 5th Earl discovered the tomb of Tutankhamun and there is a special Egyptian exhibition. Open 6th Jul-5th Sept, Tues-Fri and Sun, 11am-5pm. Phone for Bank Hol openings. Schools Price B.

New Milton, **Sammy Miller Museum,** Bashley Cross Roads, www.sammymiller.co.uk 01425 620777. A large motor cycle collection in an attractive courtyard setting with small playground, farm animals and a tearoom. Open daily, 10am-4.30pm. Schools **Open all year** Price A/B.

Petersfield(near), **Butser Ancient Farm,** Chalton, 023 9259 8838. Learn about the everyday life of the Celts and Romans at this open-air representation of an Iron-Age farm settlement. Visitors are encouraged to try activities of the day, such as spinning, pottery, grinding corn and feeding livestock. Phone for opening times. Schools Price B.

Portchester, **Portchester Castle,** EH, 023 9237 8291, has the most complete Roman walls in Northern Europe, a Norman keep, moat, and the remains of Richard II's palace. Phone for opening details and prices. Schools.

Portsmouth, **Charles Dickens Birthplace,** 393 Old Commercial Road, 023 9282 7261. The house has been restored in the Regency style appropriate to Dickens' parents. Open daily, Apr-Sept, 10am-5.30pm, Oct, 5pm. Schools Price A.
Historic Dockyard, Victory Gate, www.historicdockyard.co.uk 023 9286 1512. See three of the world's greatest historic ships: HMS Victory, HMS Warrior, and the Mary Rose. Action Stations brings the modern high-tech Royal Navy within reach of the public. Visit the Royal Naval Museum and children can let off steam in the Fighting Top Playship in Boathouse No. 7. Open daily, Apr-Oct, 10am-5.30pm, Nov-Mar, 10am-5pm. All-inclusive ticket valid for all attractions. Schools **Open all year** Price E.

Rockbourne, **Rockbourne Roman Villa,** 01725 518541. Once a 40-room villa, the modern museum building has pictorial scenes of villa life and displays of Roman artefacts. School workshops available, phone for details. Open daily, Apr-Sept, 10.30am-6pm. Schools Price A.

Romsey, **Broadlands,** www.broadlands.net 01794 505010, famous as the home of Lord Mountbatten, is an elegant Palladian mansion in a beautiful landscaped setting on the banks of the River Test. Children under 12 accompanied by parent/guardian admitted free. Open weekdays only, end Jun-end Aug, 1-5.30pm. Fuller details available from the website. Schools Price B/C.
King John's House, 01794 512200, is a restored 13th-century upper hall house, close to Romsey Abbey, with a rare bone floor and medieval graffiti! Enjoy a mini wildlife trail around the house and visit the Heritage Centre. Open Apr-Sept, Mon-Sat, 10am-4pm. Heritage Centre open all year. Schools Price A.

Selborne, Gilbert White's House and Garden and the Oates Museum, 01420 511275, was the 18th-century home of the author of 'The Natural History of Selborne'. Open daily, 11am-5pm. Museum undergoing refurbishment, phone for re-opening details. Gardens open daily and throughout refurbishment. Schools Open all year Price A.

Sherborne St John, The Vyne, NT, 01256 881337. Woodland walks and lawns sloping to the lake provide a magnificent setting for this early Tudor house which offers an insight into the 500-year development of country house architecture, interior design and taste. Children's trails and family events. House open: 20th Mar-31st Oct, Mon-Wed, 1-5pm, Sat-Sun, 11am-5pm. Grounds: 11am-5pm. Schools Price B Check out page 22.

Southampton, Medieval Merchants House, French Street, EH, 023 8022 1503. Formerly the home of a wine merchant, this timber-framed house has been refurbished to recreate a 13th-century town house and shop. Open daily, Apr-Sept, 10am-6pm, Oct, 5pm. Schools Price A.

Southsea, Cumberland House, Eastern Parade, 023 9282 7261, has many imaginative and informative displays depicting local natural history for children to enjoy, from dinosaurs to birdwatching. Visit the butterfly house Apr-Sept. Open daily, Apr-Sept, 10am-5.30pm, Oct-Mar, 10am-5pm. Up to 2 children under 13 free. Schools Open all year Price A.
D-Day Museum, Clarence Esplanade, 023 9282 7261. The Overlord Embroidery, with multi-language 'Soundalive' commentary, depicts the events of D-Day. Other displays enable you to experience the sights and sounds of Britain at War. 'D-Day 60' events and commemorations in 2004. Open daily, Apr-Sept, 10am-5.30pm, Oct-Mar, 10am-5pm. Schools Open all year Price B.
The Royal Marines Museum, www.royalmarinesmuseum.co.uk 023 9281 9385. The 300-year history of the Royal Marines told through exciting interactive displays and exhibits. New for 2004 D-Day exhibition. Open daily, Whitsun-Aug, 10am-5pm, Sept-May, 10am-4.30pm. Schools Open all year Price B.
Southsea Castle, 023 9282 7261, was built in 1544 by Henry VIII. An audio-visual presentation of the history of the castle sets the scene for exploring the keep and underground tunnels. Enter the 'Time Tunnel' for audio-visual scenes from the castle's past. Open daily, Apr-Oct, 10am-5.30pm, Oct, 5pm. Up to 2 children under 13 free. Schools Price A.

Stratfield Saye, Stratfield Saye House, 01256 882882, home to the Dukes of Wellington since 1817. House and gardens offer insight into the life of the Great Duke. Open 9th Apr-12th Apr, 6th Jul-1st Aug, 11.30am-last admission 3.30pm. Schools Price B.

Totton, Eling Tide Mill, Eling Toll Bridge, www.elingtidemill.org.uk 023 8086 9575. See natural tide power harnessed in the only surviving tide mill in the regular production of wholemeal flour. Phone for milling times. Open Wed-Sun and Bank Hol Mons, 10am-4pm. Schools Open all year Price A.

Whitchurch, Whitchurch Silk Mill, 28 Winchester Street, 01256 892065, is the oldest silk weaving mill in Britain, and now a working museum. There are children's quiz sheets and the opportunity to have a go at weaving. Riverside garden with ducks and trout. Children's activities in school hols. Open Tues-Sun and Bank Hols, 10.30am-5pm. Schools Open all year Price A.

Winchester, The Gurkha Museum, Peninsula Barracks, Romsey Road, 01962 843659, commemorates the services of the Gurkhas to the British since 1815. Open Mon-Sat, 10am-4.30pm, Sun, 12noon-4pm. Schools Open all year Price A.
Intech, Hampshire Technology Centre, Telegraph Way, on B3404, www.intech2000.co.uk 01962 863791. An opportunity for children to explore, discover and be challenged by the world of science and technology in this hands-on interactive centre. Open daily, 10am-4pm. Special school group concessions. Schools Open all year Price B.

Royal Green Jackets Museum, Peninsula Barracks, Romsey Road, www.rgjassociation.org.uk 01962 828549. This fine regimental museum tells the history of the nation and its regiments from 1741. Open Mon-Sat, 10am-1pm and 2-5pm, Sun, 12noon-4pm. Schools Open all year Price A.

Winchester City Mill, NT, 01962 870057, is a water-powered corn mill in the city centre with hands-on milling activities for children. See the restored machinery and exhibition display, experience the awesome power of river water and visit the island garden. Family quiz available and lots of children's activities during school holidays. Open 6th Mar-28th Mar, Sat-Sun, 11am-5pm; 1st Apr-27th Jun, 8th Sept-31st Oct, Wed-Sun, 11am-5pm; 30th Jun-5th Sept, daily, 11am-5pm, 1st Nov-23rd Dec, daily, 11am-4pm. Schools Price A Check out page 22.

SALISBURY AREA

Amesbury(near), **Stonehenge,** EH, 01980 624715 (Information line). Perpetual mystery surrounds these famous stones on Salisbury Plain. Open daily, times vary. Schools Open all year Price B.

Salisbury, **Discover Salisbury,** at The Medieval Hall, The Close, www.medieval-hall.co.uk 01722 324731. The big-screen presentation lasts 40 minutes and describes Salisbury's past and then the area as it is today. Open Apr-Sept, daily (telephone to confirm), and all year for pre-booked groups. Schools Price A.

Mompesson House, NT, The Close, 01722 335659. An early 18th-century house with beautiful interiors. There is a children's guide with quiz. Open 9th Apr-31st Oct, Sat-Wed, 11am-5pm. Schools Price A.

Old Sarum, EH, 01722 335398. Originally a huge Iron-Age hill fort, the ruins leave plenty of room for the imagination. Telephone for opening times. Schools Open all year Price A.

Redcoats in The Wardrobe Museum, 58 The Close, www.thewardrobe.org.uk 01722 419419, houses the Berkshire and Wiltshire regimental collections. Find out about global exploits and tackle a Redcoats Mission quiz sheet. Open Apr-Oct, daily, 10am-5pm, Nov-early Dec and early Feb-Mar, Tues-Sun. Schools Price A.

Salisbury and South Wiltshire Museum, The King's House, 65 The Close, www.salisburymuseum.org.uk 01722 332151. Imaginative displays cover prehistory, Old Sarum, Romans, Saxons and local history. Try out the interactive exhibits in the redesigned Stonehenge Gallery. Open Mon-Sat, 10am-5pm, and Jul-Aug only, Suns, 2-5pm. Schools Open all year Price A.

Tisbury(near), **Old Wardour Castle,** EH, 01747 870487. A picture-book setting with plenty of scope for pretend play. This is a very child-friendly site with information panels and a free children's leaflet. Telephone for opening times. Schools Open all year Price A.

Wilton, **Wilton Carpet Factory,** Minster Street, www.wiltoncarpets.com 01722 742890. An opportunity to tour a modern working factory, see the looms in action and find out how carpets are made. A museum on site shows the history of Wilton. Telephone for factory tour information. Schools Open all year Price A.

Wilton House, www.wiltonhouse.com 01722 746729, has 450 years of fascinating history and a fine art collection. In the Old Riding School are the recreated Tudor Kitchen and Victorian Laundry. Quiz sheets, landscaped parkland and a massive adventure playground. Open 2nd Apr-31st Oct, daily, 10.30am-5.30pm. House (only) closed Mons, but open Bank Hols. Schools Birthdays Price C.

ISLE OF WIGHT

Alum Bay, The Needles Old Battery, NT, West High Down, 01983 754772, is a cliff-top Victorian fort with stunning views and two original cannons. Follow the secret tunnel which leads to a unique bird's eye view of The Needles. Enjoy the exhibition in the 'Gunpowder Magazine' and the children's display in the 'Shell Store'. Open 28th Mar-30th Jun, Sept-Oct, Sat-Thurs, 10.30am-5pm. Open daily, Jul-Aug. Schools   Price B   Check out page 22.

Bembridge, Bembridge Windmill, NT, Mill Road, 01983 873945, is the only surviving windmill on the island and dates from around 1700. Much of the wooden machinery is still intact and there is access to the upper floor. Open 29th Mar-29th Oct, Sun-Fri, 10am-5pm. Open daily, Jul-Aug, 10am-5pm. Schools   Price A   Check out page 22.

Heritage Centre, Church Road, www.bembridge.org 01983 873606, is set in a former Victorian school and has photos and artefacts from past and present village life. For older children. Open May-Sept, Mon, Wed and Fri, 10am-4pm, Sat, 10am-12noon. Schools   Price A.

Isle of Wight Shipwreck Centre, Sherbourne Street, 01983 872223. Discover the narwhal tusk and Marmaduke the Merman and other artefacts from local shipwrecks. Open Apr-Oct, 10am-5pm. Schools   Price A.

Brading, Brading Roman Villa, Morton Old Road, near Sandown, 01983 406223. Museum closed for refurbishment. Mosaics re-opening for viewing Aug 2004. Viewing platform and presentations on DVD available from Easter. Ring for opening details. Schools   Price A.

Isle of Wight Wax Works, 46 High Street, www.iwwaxworks.co.uk 01983 407286. Many realistic waxworks on offer, and Chamber of Horrors in the dungeon. Open daily, 10am-5pm. Schools   Open all year   Price B/C.

Lilliput Antique Doll and Toy Museum, High Street, www.lilliputmuseum.com 01983 407231. Open daily, 10am-5pm. Schools   Open all year   Price A.

Morton Manor, 01983 406168, is a charming family home rebuilt in 1680. Garden, vineyard, lake, play area and small museum. Open Easter-Oct, Sun-Fri, 10am-5.30pm. Schools   Price B.

Calbourne, Calbourne Water Mill and Rural Museum, near Newport, www.calbournewatermill.co.uk 01983 531227. A working water mill with milling at 3pm weekdays. Ten-acre grounds for walks, picnics and a bouncy galleon for under 10s, as well as putting green and punts (extra charges apply). Open Easter-Oct, 10am-5pm. Schools   Price B.

Carisbrooke, Carisbrooke Castle, EH, near Newport, 01983 522107. Climb the keep, discover the well house and enjoy the museum housed in the medieval Great Hall with interactive exhibitions and costumed guided tours. Phone for opening details and prices. Schools.

Cowes, Isle of Wight Model Railways, The Parade, 01983 280111. Large railway layouts, including the 'Rocky Mountains'; low push buttons for toddlers. Open daily, Apr-Sept, 11am-5pm, Oct-Mar, Mon-Sat only. Schools   Open all year   Price A.

East Cowes(near), Osborne House, EH, 01983 200022. At Queen Victoria's seaside home explore the Swiss-style playhouse and take a carriage ride through the grounds. Phone for opening details and prices. Schools.

Godshill, Model Village, High Street, 01983 840270. Become Gulliver and look down upon this miniature world. Stone houses with real thatched roofs and tiny gardens. Open Mar-Oct, 10.30am. Call for varying closing times. Price A.

Natural History Centre, High Street, www.shellmuseum.co.uk 01983 840333, has over 40,000 sea shells. See a collection of fossils, minerals and gem stones. Gift shop. Open daily, 10am-5pm. Schools   Open all year   Price A.

Nostalgia Toy Museum, High Street, 01983 840181, has a collection of Matchbox, Dinky and Corgi vehicles dating from 1930-1970, Star Wars toys and more. Open daily, Easter-Oct, 10am-5pm. Schools   Price A.

Newport, Classic Boat Museum, The Quay, Newport Harbour, 01983 533493. See over 50 motor and sailing boats, some historical. Open daily, Easter-Oct, 10.30am-4.30pm, Tues and Sun only in Winter. **Schools Open all year Price A.**

Isle of Wight Bus and Coach Museum, The Quay, Newport Harbour, 01983 533352, where you will find vintage buses housed in a former grain store. Climb aboard and explore! Displays and shop. Open 4th Apr-30th Sept, Tues-Thurs, Sat, Sun, 10.30am-4pm; Easter hols, Summer half-term and 25th Jul-5th Sept, open daily; Oct, Sun and Tues. **Schools Price A.**

Museum of Island History, High Street, 01983 823433. Hands-on exhibits, touch-screen computers, quizzes and games connected to the heritage of the island. Open daily, Mon-Sat, 9.30am-5.30pm, Sun, 10am-4pm. **Schools Open all year Price A.**

Newport Ghost Walk, The Wheatsheaf Hotel, St Thomas' Square, 01983 823366, is presented in a theatrical way. Learn how people lived on the island, as you walk along historic streets and alleys. Phone for times and price.

Roman Villa, Cypress Road, 01983 823433. Discover the intricacies of Roman bath time, the garden and many artefacts. Open Apr-Oct, Mon-Sat, 10am-4.30pm. Open some Suns in Jul and Aug. **Schools Price A.**

Newtown, Old Town Hall & Nature Reserve, NT, Mill Road, 01983 531785, was the setting for often turbulent elections in the early 20th century. An exhibition depicts the exploits of 'Ferguson's Gang'. Wading birds and over-wintering birds can be seen at the Nature Reserve, which is always accessible. Open 29th Mar-30th Jun, Mon, Wed, Sun, 2-5pm; Jul-Aug, Sun-Thurs, 2-5pm; 1st Sept-20th Oct, Mon, Wed, Sun, 2-5pm. **Schools Price A Check out page 22.**

Sandown, Dinosaur Isle, Culver Parade, www.dinosaurisle.com 01983 404344. Enter a 'Pterosaur' shaped building and discover unique dinosaur relics, sounds and even smells! Take a trip through the fossilised time tunnel, stepping back 125 million years, and see life-sized dinosaur models including an Animatronic Neovenator. Guided Fossil Walks can be pre-booked (additional charge) and are usually held in high season and school holidays, or by pre-arrangement for schools. Activity sheets and a Teacher's Guide are available and there are Guided Talks and a Fossil Identification Service. In the Education Room there are themed displays at various times throughout the year. Open daily, Apr-Oct, 10am-6pm, Nov-Mar, 4pm. **Schools Open all year Price B Check out page 22.**

Ventnor, Coastal Visitors Centre, www.coastalwight.gov.uk 01983 855400. Discover facts about the island and identify local species in the Aquarium. Open Mon-Sat, 9.30am-5pm. **Schools Open all year Price A.**

Ventnor(near), Smuggling Museum, Ventnor Botanic Garden, Undercliff Drive, on the A3055, 01983 853677. Enter underground vaults and discover the ingenuity of smugglers over the past 700 years. Open daily, Apr-Sept, 10am-5pm (last admission). **Price A.**

Wroxall, Appuldurcombe House, EH, Appuldurcombe Road. www.appuldurcombe.co.uk 01983 840188. A partly restored 18th-century baroque house with grounds designed by Capability Brown. Check out 'Farms'. Phone for opening details and prices. **Schools.**

Yarmouth, Yarmouth Castle, EH, 01983 760678. Watch the yachts pass through the Solent from the battlements of Henry VIII's final fortress. Phone for opening details and prices. **Schools.**

Yarmouth(near), Island Planetarium, Fort Victoria, off A3054, www.islandastronomy.co.uk 01983 761555 or 0800 195 8295. Journey to the edge of the universe and have fun in the exhibition area. Open daily in school hols, Easter-Oct, midday showings in term time. **Schools Price A.**

Model Railway, Victoria Station, Fort Victoria, off A3054, www.fortvictoria.co.uk 01983 761553, is computer controlled. Take personal control for an additional charge. Open daily, Easter-Sept, (Sat-Sun and daily over half-term, Oct), 10am-5pm. **Price B.**

Sports & Leisure

Sport is a great way for young people to channel surplus energy or occupy spare time. Not only does it offer personal challenge, foster team spirit and generate an interest which can provide a pleasurable and necessary diversion in later life, sport is also a good way to have fun, make new friends, to be fit and feel good. Test the water with the numerous watersports available or try ice skating, snow sports or the many different activities on offer at your sports and leisure centre.

Leisure pursuits may lead to a new hobby or simply occupy leisure time in a relaxed and entertaining way. Have a go at pottery painting, visit the theatre or go bowling with the family.

Abbreviations: A: Archery, Ab: Abseiling, AT: Aerial Trekking, C: Canoeing, CCn: Canadian Canoes, Cl: Climbing, Cm: Camping, Cv: Caving, DB: Dragon Boating, E: Environmental Studies, F: Fencing, HR: High Ropes, JS: Jet Skiing, K: Kayaking, KS: Kite Surfing, LR: Low Ropes, MA: Multi-activity Days, MB: Mountain Biking, Mt: Mountaineering, O: Orienteering, PB: Power Boating, PS: Problem Solving, Q: Quad Biking, R: Riding, RBd: Raft Building, Ri: Ringoes, S: Sailing, Sb: Snowboarding, Sf: Surfing, Sn: Snorkelling, TB: Team Building, Tn: Tunnelling, Tu: Tubing, W: Windsurfing, Wb: Wakeboarding, WS: Water Skiing, Z: Zipwire.

ADVENTURE ACTIVITIES

DORSET: Christchurch: Avon Tyrrell Activity & Residential Centre Bransgore 01425 672347 A Ab HR LR PS TB. **Langton Matravers: Leeson House Field Studies Centre** 01929 422126 E O PS. **Poole: Hamworthy Outdoor Education Centre** Lulworth Ave 01202 678336 Ab C Cl Cv K Mt MB O PS S. **Ringwood(near): Go Ape!** Moors Valley Country Pk 0870 444 5562 AT. **Southbourne: Hengistbury Head Centre** Broadway 01202 425173 E K O PS S. **Wareham: Carey Outdoor Education Centre** 01929 552265 Cm E LR O PS. **Weymouth: Weymouth Outdoor Education Centre** Knightsdale Rd 01305 784927 A Ab Cl Cv K O PS S TB.
HAMPSHIRE: Brockenhurst: Tile Barn Outdoor Education Centre Church Hill 01590 623160 LR MB O PS TB. **Calshot: Activities Centre** 023 8089 2077 A Ab C Cl HR LR MB O PS Sb TB W. **Curdridge: Fairthorne Manor YMCA** 01489 785228 A C Cl K O. **Eastleigh: Marwell Activity Centre** Hurst La Fishers Pond 01962 777547 A C Cl HR MA O Q. **Portsmouth: The Peter Ashley Activity Centres** Fort Purbrook and Fort Widley Portsdown Hill Rd 023 9232 1223 A C Cl PS R. **Southampton: Woodmill Outdoor Centre** 023 8055 5993 A C Cl E HR LR MA O PS Tn Z.
ISLE OF WIGHT: Bembridge: Camp Beaumont 01603 284280 A Cl Cv E F HR K LR O PS Q R Sf, **Kingswood Centre** (schools only) Old School Building Hill Way 01983 875353 A Cl Cv E F HR K LR O PS Q R. **Bonchurch: East Dene Centre** 01983 852374 A E O PS. **Newport: Medina Valley Centre** Dodnor La 01983 522195 A E O PS. **Wootton: 3D Education & Adventure** Little Canada Centre New Rd 01983 885400 A Ab Cl E F HR O PS TB Z.

BALLOON RIDES

DORSET: Bournemouth: Bournemouth Eye Balloon Lower Gdns 01202 314539. A tethered balloon, rising 150m (weather permitting).

BOWLING (TEN PIN)

DORSET: Bournemouth: Super Bowl Glenfern Rd 01202 291717. **Poole: Bowlplex** Poole Rd Branksome 01202 765489, **Megabowl** Tower Pk 01202 715907. **Weymouth: Bowlings** The Excise House Hope Sq 01305 760706, **Lakeside Superbowl** St Nicholas St 01305 781444.
HAMPSHIRE: Aldershot: Aldershot Bowling Hippodrome Hse Birchett Rd 01252 336844. **Andover: Breakers** Bridge St 01264 324072. **Basingstoke: Bowlplex** Leisure Pk 01256 811405. **Fareham: Go Bowling** Newgate La 01329 287808. **Havant: Bowlplex** Portsdown Hill

Rd 023 9245 4888. Portsmouth: **AMF Bowling** Arundel St 023 9282 0505. Southampton: **AMF Bitterne Bowl** Bitterne Village 023 8044 7742, **Hot Shots Leisure World** West Quay Rd (families until 8pm only) 023 8033 3003, **Megabowl** Aukland Rd Millbrook 023 8051 1511.
SALISBURY AREA: Salisbury: **Strikers** (at Outburst) Unit 5 Milford Trading Est Blakey Rd 01722 413121.
ISLE OF WIGHT: Ryde: **L.A. Bowl** The Pavilion Esplanade 01983 617070. Sandown: **Superbowl** 01983 406701.

BRASS RUBBING

HAMPSHIRE: Winchester: **Westgate Museum** High St 01962 869864.
ISLE OF WIGHT: Arreton: **Brass Rubbing Centre** Coach House St George's Church 01983 526290.

CINEMAS

DORSET: Bournemouth: **ABC Film Centre** Westover Rd 0870 900 7694, **Odeon* Cinema** Westover Rd, **Sheridan Imax® Centre** 01202 200000. Christchurch: **Regent Centre** 51 High St 01202 499148. Dorchester: **Plaza Cinema** Trinity St 01305 262488. Lyme Regis: **Regent Cinema** Broad St 01297 442053. Poole: **Lighthouse Poole Centre for the Arts** Kingland Rd 01202 685222, **UCI Cinemas** Tower Pk Mannings Heath 0870 010 2030. Swanage: **The Mowlem Theatre** Shore Rd 01929 422239. Wareham: **The Rex** West St 01929 552778. Weymouth: **Cineworld** New Bond St 0871 220 8000.
HAMPSHIRE: Alton: **Palace Cinema** Normandy St 01420 82303. Basingstoke: **Warner Village** Basingstoke Leisure Pk 0870 240 6020. Cosham: **Carlton Cinema** High St 023 9237 6635. Lymington: **Centre Cinema** Community Centre New St 01590 676939. Portsmouth: **Odeon* Cinema** London Rd, **UCI Cinema** Port Solent 0870 010 2030, Warner Village Portsmouth Harbour 0870 240 6020. Southampton: **Harbour Lights Cinema** Ocean Village 023 8033 5533, **Odeon* Cinema** West Quay Rd, **UGC Cinema** Ocean Village 0870 155 5132. Winchester: **The Screen** Southgate St 01962 856009.
SALISBURY AREA: Salisbury: **Odeon*** New Canal.
ISLE OF WIGHT: Newport: **Cineworld** Coppins Bridge 01983 537570, **Medina Theatre** Mountbatten Centre Fairlee Rd 01983 527020. Ryde: **Commodore Cinema** Star St 01983 565609.

* ODEON CINEMAS Hotline: 0870 5050007

CLIMBING CENTRE (INDOOR)

ISLE OF WIGHT: Newport: **Medina Leisure Centre** Fairlee Rd (classes for 8-16 year olds) 01983 523767.

CRAZY GOLF

DORSET: Bournemouth: Boscombe Gardens, Bournemouth Gardens, Hengistbury Head, Tuckton Tea Gardens. Lyme Regis: Lister Gardens. Poole: Poole Park, Sandbanks. Swanage: The Bandstand. Warmwell: Warmwell Leisure Centre. Weymouth: Weymouth Beach.
HAMPSHIRE: Andover: Charlton Lakeside Pavilion. Basingstoke: Eastrop Park Eastrop Way. Lee-on-Solent: Marine Parade West. Riseley: Wellington Country Park. Southampton: Bassett Sports Centre. Southsea: Canoe Lake The Common.
SALISBURY AREA: Salisbury: Victoria Park Castle Rd.
ISLE OF WIGHT: Ryde: **Puckpool Park** 01983 562086. Sandown: **Sandham Gardens** Culver Pde 01983 402747. Shanklin: **Rylstone Gardens**, Shanklin Esplanade Golf 01983 863744.

Sports & Leisure

FOSSIL HUNTING

ISLE OF WIGHT: Brighstone(near): **Dinosaur Farm** Military Rd 07970 626456. Sandown: **Dinosaur Isle** Culver Pde 01983 404344.

ICE SKATING

HAMPSHIRE: Basingstoke: **Planet Ice** Basingstoke Leisure Pk 01256 355266. Gosport: **Ice Rink** Forest Way Fareham Rd 023 9251 1217.
ISLE OF WIGHT: Ryde: **Planet Ice** Quay Rd 01983 615155.

KARTING

DORSET: Christchurch: **Indoor Karting Centre** 01202 570022.
HAMPSHIRE: Aldershot: **Go-Karting for Fun** Government Rd Industrial Pk 0870 6000 601. Andover: **Go-Karting for Fun** 282 Weyhill Rd 0870 6000 601. Eastleigh: **Go-Karting for Fun** Chickenhall La 0870 6000 601. Ringwood: **Arrive and Drive Fun Karts** Ringwood Raceway Hurn Rd 01425 473305.
SALISBURY AREA: Salisbury(near): **Avago Karting** West Dean 01794 884693.
ISLE OF WIGHT: Sandown: Sandham Rides Fort St 01983 406600. Shanklin: **Esplanade** 01983 867557.

MUSIC AND MOVEMENT

Jo Jingles, www.jojingles.co.uk 01494 719360, is a leading music and singing experience with an educational slant for children aged 6 months to 7 years. Exciting and stimulating classes run at venues all over the country. For details on classes in your area or for information on the franchise opportunity please call 01494 719360, email: headoffice@jojingles.co.uk or visit the website. Birthdays Check out page 34.

Monkey Music, www.monkeymusic.co.uk 01582 766464, runs music classes for babies and children aged between 6 months and 4 years at venues all over the UK. Please telephone for details of local classes. Birthdays Check out page 34.

PITCH AND PUTT

DORSET: Bournemouth: Hengistbury Head, Solent Meads. Bridport: West Bay. Christchurch: Christchurch Quay, Two Riversmeet Leisure Centre. Swanage: Victoria Ave. Weymouth: Lodmoor Country Park.
HAMPSHIRE: Andover: Charlton Lakeside Pavilion. Basingstoke: Golf Centre Worting Rd. Fawley: Newlands Rd. Fleet: Calthorpe Park. Hayling Island: Seafront. Southampton: Riverside Park Weston Shore. Southsea: The Common (8-12s accompanied by adult only), St Helens (over 12s only). Titchfield: Titchfield Abbey Golf & Fishing 01329 846606.
ISLE OF WIGHT: Alum Bay: **Needles** View Pitch and Putt. Ryde: Appley Park 01983 402447. Sandown: Browns Culver Pde 01983 402447.

PARTY IDEA

DORSET: Bournemouth: **The Face Place,** 01202 419424, offers an exciting mobile makeover party package for girls at your party venue. Extras include hair accessories, party bags, craft or bead making and optional dressing up. Check out page 40.

POTTERY PAINTING

HAMPSHIRE: Winchester: **The Pottery Café,** Parchment Street, www.thepotterycafe.co.uk 01962 853744, is a relaxing environment and an ideal venue for parties where you can paint your own design on ready-made pottery. All ages can enjoy 90 minutes of creative fun and paint the perfect present. Fully trained staff are on hand to help

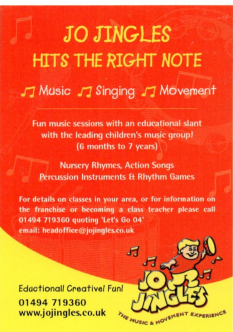

OPEN AIR SEA WATER
SWIMMING POOL

BATH ROAD, LYMINGTON

Boats, Canoes and
Sun Loungers for hire
Children's Paddling Pool
Kiosk with riverside terrace
Hot and Cold Refreshment
Sweets & ice Cream

Kiosk open from Easter until October
Pool open daily from May to September

*For further information contact the
Baths Manager, telephone: 01590 674865*

achieve amazing results. Once the chosen item is decorated, it is glazed, fired and can be collected within 10 days. All pots are dishwasher, microwave and oven safe. Services include children's parties, painting baby's hand and footprints onto pottery and late nights Weds. Booking essential during holiday times. Beverages and cakes available. **Birthdays** **Open all year** Check out page 34.

DORSET: Poole: **Poole Pottery** The Quay 01202 668681.
HAMPSHIRE: Southampton: **The Crockery** 83 Queensway 023 8063 4466. Weyhill: **Cherished China** Fairground Industrial Estate 01264 772000. Winchester: **The Pottery Café** Parchment St 01962 853744.
SALISBURY AREA: Salisbury: **Splash of Colour** 72 Fisherton St 01722 322250.
ISLE OF WIGHT: Chessell: **Chessell Pottery** Brook Rd 01983 531248.

PUTTING GREENS

DORSET: Bournemouth: Fisherman's Walk, Hengistbury Head, Tuckton Tea Gardens. Bridport: West Bay. Poole: Poole Park, Sandbanks. Swanage: Beach Gardens. Weymouth: Bowleaze Cove, Green Hill.
HAMPSHIRE: Basingstoke: Golf Centre Worting Rd. Eastleigh: Passfield Ave. Romsey: Memorial Park. Southampton: Bassett Sports Centre, Central Parks, Mayflower Park.
ISLE OF WIGHT: Cowes: Northwood Park Ward Ave 01983 280525. Ryde: Puckpool Park 01983 562086. Sandown: Browns Golf Course Culver Pde 01983 402447, Sandham Gardens Culver Pde 01983 402747. Shanklin: Esplanade Golf 01983 863744. Ventnor: Ventnor Park Park Ave 01983 855623.

QUAD BIKING

DORSET: Dorchester(near): **Henley Hillbillies** Buckland Newton (off-road adventure vehicles) 01300 345293.
HAMPSHIRE: Andover: **Quad Squad** The Mervyn Anstie Off-Road and Quad Bike Centre 01264 334293.

SKATEBOARDING

DORSET: Bournemouth: **Slades Farm** Slades Farm Rd. Bridport: **Plottingham Playing Fields**.
HAMPSHIRE: Aldershot: Manor Park. Chandlers Ford: The Knightwood Leisure Centre Valley Pk. Farnborough: Westmead. Hythe: Forest Front, Jones La. Romsey: The Rapids. Southsea: Southsea Common. West Totton: Bartley Park.
SALISBURY AREA: Salisbury: Churchill Gardens Southampton Rd.
ISLE OF WIGHT: Cowes: Cowes Skate Park Cowes Recreation Centre. East Cowes: East Cowes Park. Newport: Seaclose Skate Park Seaclose Pk. Ryde: Sea Front.

SNOWSPORTS

DORSET: Hurn: **Christchurch Ski Centre** Matchams La 01202 499155. Warmwell: **Warmwell Leisure Resort** 01305 852911.
HAMPSHIRE: Aldershot: **Alpine Snowsports** Gallwey Rd 01252 325889. Calshot: **Calshot Activities Centre** 023 8089 2077. Southampton: **Southampton Alpine Centre** Sports Centre Bassett 023 8079 0970.

SPORTING AND ARTS EVENTS

ISLE OF WIGHT: Ryde: **Smallbrook Speedway Stadium** Ashley Rd 01983 811180, **Waltzing Waters** Water, Light & Music Spectacular Westridge Centre 01983 811333.

SPORTS AND LEISURE CENTRES

Abbreviations: LC: Leisure Centre, RC: Recreation Centre, SC: Sports Centre. * Centre has a swimming pool.
DORSET: Blandford Forum: **Blandford LC*** Milldown Rd 01258 455566. Bournemouth: **Littledown Centre*** Chaseside Castle La 01202 417600. Bridport: **Bridport LC*** Brewery Fields 01308 427464. Christchurch: **Two Riversmeet LC*** Stony Lane South 01202 477987. Dorchester: **Thomas Hardy LC*** Coburg Rd 01305 266772. Ferndown: **Ferndown LC*** Cherry Grove 01202 877468. Gillingham: **Gillingham LC*** Harding La 01747 822026. Poole: **Ashdown LC** Adastral Rd Canford Heath 01202 604224, **Broadstone LC*** Station Approach 01202 777766, **Poole SC** The Dolphin Centre 01202 777788, **Rossmore LC*** Herbert Ave Parkstone 01202 738787. Shaftesbury: **Motcombe Park SC** 01747 856317, **Shaftesbury LC** Salisbury Rd 01747 854637. Sherborne: **The Gryphon LC** Bristol Rd 01935 814011. Verwood: **LC Chiltern** Dri 01202 826560. Wareham: **Purbeck SC*** Worgret Rd 01929 556454. Weymouth: **Weymouth SC** Redlands Dorchester Rd 01305 813113. Wimborne: **Queen Elizabeth LC*** Blandford Rd 01202 888208.
HAMPSHIRE: Aldershot: **Connaught LC** Tongham Rd 01252 344438. Alton: **SC*** Chawton Park Rd 01420 82772. Andover: **Andover LC*** West St 01264 324144. Basingstoke: **Basingstoke SC*** Festival Pl 01256 326331. Baughurst: **The Hurst Centre** Brimpton Rd 01734 811611. Bordon: **Mill Chase LC*** Mill Chase Rd 01420 472549. Calshot: **Activities Centre** Calshot Spit 023 8089 2077. Chandlers Ford: **The Knightwood LC** Skys Wood Rd Valley Pk 023 8027 6254. Charlton: **Lakeside** West Portway 01264 338759. Dibden Purlieu: **Applemore RC*** Claypits La 023 8084 4288. Eastleigh: **Fleming Park LC*** Passfield Ave 023 8064 1555. Fareham: **Fareham LC*** Park La 01329 233652. Farnborough: **Farnborough RC*** Westmead 01252 370411. Fawley: **Gang Warily Community Centre** Newlands Rd 023 8089 3603. Fleet: **Hart LC*** Hitches La 01252 629974. Fordingbridge: **Forest Edge LC*** Sandy Balls Holiday Centre 01425 651216. Gosport: **Holbrook RC*** Fareham Rd 023 9252 2532, **St Vincent LC*** Mill La 023 9252 3451. Havant: **Horizon Havant LC*** Civic Centre Rd 023 9247 6026. Hedge End: **Wildern SC*** Wildern La 01489 787128. Liphook: **Bohunt Community Centre** Longmore Rd 01428 724324. Lymington: **Lymington RC*** North St Pennington 01590 670333. New Milton: **New Milton RC*** Gore Rd 01425 617441. Petersfield: **Taro LC*** Penns Pl 01730 263 996. Portsmouth: **The Mountbatten Centre** Alexandra Pk 023 9269 0011, **St Luke's SC*** Greetham St 023 9283 8798. Ringwood: **Ringwood RC*** Parsonage Barn La 01425 478813. Romsey: **Romsey SC** Lower Southampton Rd 01794 515103. Southampton: **Bitterne LC*** Dean Rd 023 8043 7647, **St Mary's LC** St Mary's Rd 023 8022 7579, **Southampton SC** Thornhill Rd Bassett 023 8079 0693. Southsea: **Wimbledon Park SC** Taswell Rd 023 9282 5075. Totton: **Totton RC*** Water La 023 8086 7474. Waterlooville: **Horizon LC** Waterberry Dri 023 9223 1010. Whitchurch: **Testbourne Campus** Micheldever Rd 01256 892261. Winchester: River Park LC* Gordon Rd 01962 848700. Yateley: **Frogmore LC** Potley Hill Rd 01252 873454.
SALISBURY AREA: Downton: **Downton LC** Wick La 01725 513668. Salisbury: **Five Rivers LC*** The Butts Hulse Rd 01722 339966. Tisbury: **Tisbury & District SC** Weaveland Rd 01747 871141.
ISLE OF WIGHT: Freshwater: **West Wight SC*** 01983 752168. Newport: **Medina LC*** 01983 523767. Sandown: **The Heights LC*** 01983 405594.

SWIMMING POOLS (INDOOR)

Please also check the list of Sports & Leisure Centres above. Those marked with an * have a pool.
DORSET: Bournemouth: **Kinson Swimming Pool** South Kinson Dri 01202 575555, **Stokewood Swimming Pool and Fitness Centre** Stokewood Rd 01202 529658. Poole: **Dolphin Pool** Kingland Rd 01202 677217. Weymouth: **Weymouth & Portland Swimming Pool** Knightsdale Rd 01305 774373.

HAMPSHIRE: Basingstoke: **Aquadrome** Basingstoke Leisure Pk 01256 472343. Portsmouth: **Victoria Swimming Centre** Anglesey Rd 023 9282 3822. Romsey: **Romsey Leisure Centre** Southampton Rd 01794 830333. Southampton: **Oaklands Pool** Fairisle Rd Lordshill 023 8074 1414, **The Quays** Harbour Parade 023 8072 0900. Tadley: **Tadley Swimming Pool** New Rd 0118 981 7818.
SALISBURY AREA: Durrington: **Durrington Swimming Pool** Recreation Rd 01980 594594.
ISLE OF WIGHT: Ryde: **Ryde Waterside Pool** Esplanade 01983 563656.

SWIMMING POOLS (OUTDOOR)

HAMPSHIRE: Lymington: **Open Air Sea Water Pool,** Bath Road, 01590 674865/676009, is one of the largest open air pools on the south coast (90m by 30m) and overlooks The Needles on the Isle of Wight. Children can bring along inflatables and play under the watchful eye of fully trained lifeguards, while younger children will enjoy the small paddling pool and sandpit. In a further area, the more adventurous can hire canoes or rowing boats. Sun loungers are for hire and spectators can relax on a large patio area. The adjoining kiosk sells snacks and refreshments. Book the pool for a special party or a barbecue (hire after 6.30pm). Party rates and season tickets available. Open daily, May-Sept, 10am-6pm. Open subject to weather conditions, so telephone first to avoid disappointment. Schools Birthdays Price A Check out page 34.

HAMPSHIRE: Aldershot: **Pools Complex** Guildford Rd (open May-Sept) 01252 323482. Fordingbridge: **Forest Edge Leisure Centre** Sandy Balls (open May-Sept) 01425 653042. Lymington: **Lymington Open Air Sea Water Pool** Bath Rd 01590 674865/676009. Portsmouth: **Hilsea Lido** 023 9266 4608. Whitchurch: **Testbourne Campus** Micheldever Rd (open Jun-Aug) 01256 892261.
SALISBURY AREA: Tisbury: **Tisbury Outdoor Pool** Weaveland Rd.

THEATRES

Grease on Tour, www.greasethemusical.co.uk Grease the Musical is on tour throughout the country this year and is going to be at a theatre near you! The show is packed with explosive energy, vibrant 1950s pop culture and lots of unforgettable songs. Take the family to this fabulous Rock'n'Roll musical filled with irresistible groovy and memorable moments. Don't miss it! For full information, casting details, competitions, special offers and full tour venues and dates log on to the website above. **Check out page 38.**

DORSET: Blandford Forum: **Bryanston Arts Centre** 01258 456533. Bournemouth: **Bournemouth International Centre** Exeter Rd, **Pavilion Theatre** Westover Rd, **Pier Theatre** Bournemouth Pier (Summer season only) 01202 456456. Bridport: **Bridport Art Centre** South St 01308 427183. Christchurch: **Regent Centre** 51 High St 01202 499148. Dorchester: **Dorchester Arts Centre** School La 01305 266926. Poole: **Lighthouse** Poole Centre for the Arts Kingland Rd 01202 685222. Shaftesbury: **Shaftesbury Arts Centre** 13 Bell St 01747 854321. Swanage: **The Mowlem Theatre** Shore Rd 01929 422229. Weymouth: **The Weymouth Pavilion** The Esplanade 01305 783225. Wimborne: **Tivoli Theatre** West Borough 01202 885566.
HAMPSHIRE: Aldershot: **Princes Hall** Princes Way 01252 329155, **West End Centre** Queens Rd 01252 330040. Andover: **Cricklade Theatre** Charlton Rd 01264 365698. Basingstoke: **The Anvil** Churchill Way 01256 819797, **Central Studio** Queen Mary's College 01256 417511, **Haymarket Theatre** Wote St 01256 465566. Eastleigh: **The Point** Leigh Rd 023 8065 2333. Fareham: **Ashcroft Arts Centre** Osborn Rd 01329 235161, **Ferneham Hall** Osborn Rd 01329 231942. Farnborough: **Prince Regent Theatre** Guildford Rd East 01252 510859. Hayling Island: **Station Theatre** Station Rd 023 9246 6363. Havant: Havant Arts Centre East St 023 9247 2700. New Milton: **Forest Arts Centre** Old Milton Rd 01425 612393.

Sports & Leisure

Portsmouth: New Theatre Royal Guildhall Walk 023 9264 9000, **Portsmouth Arts Centre** Reginald Rd 023 9273 2236, **Portsmouth Guildhall** Guildhall Sq 023 9282 4355. **Romsey: The Plaza Theatre** Winchester Rd 01794 523054. **Southampton: The Gantry Youth Theatre** off Blechynden Tce 023 8042 2099, **Mayflower Theatre** Commercial Rd 023 8071 1811, **Nuffield Theatre** University Rd 023 8067 1771, **Turner Sims Concert Hall** University 023 8059 5151. **Southsea: Kings Theatre** Albert Rd 023 9282 8282. **Winchester: Theatre Royal** Jewry St 01962 840440, **Tower Arts Centre** King's Rd 01962 867986. **SALISBURY AREA:** Salisbury: **City Hall** Malthouse La 01722 327676, **Salisbury Arts Centre** Bedwin St 01722 321744, **Salisbury Playhouse** Malthouse La 01722 320333, **Studio Theatre** Ashley Rd 01722 338579.
ISLE OF WIGHT: Newport: **Apollo Theatre** Pyle St 01983 527267, **Medina Theatre** Mountbatten Centre Fairlee Rd 01983 527020, **Quay Arts Centre** Sea St 01983 528825. Ryde: **Ryde Theatre** Lind St 01983 568099. Shanklin: **The Portico Theatre** Priory Rd 01983 865123, **Shanklin Theatre** Prospect Rd 01983 868000. Ventnor: **The Winter Gardens** Pier St 01983 855215.

WATERSPORTS

DORSET: Poole: **Hamworthy Outdoor Education Centre** Lulworth Ave 01202 678336 C K PB S, **Poole Harbour Boardsailing** Lilliput 01202 700503 KS W, **Rockley Point Sailing School** Rockley Pk 01202 677272 PB S W. Southbourne: **Hengistbury Head Centre** Southbourne 01202 425173 C K PB S. Swanage: **Pier Head Watersports** 01929 422254 PB Ri Tu WS. Weymouth: **Weymouth Outdoor Education Centre** Knightsdale Rd 01305 784927 C CCn K S, **Windtek Windsurfing** 109 Portland Rd 01305 787900 W.
HAMPSHIRE: Calshot: **Calshot Activities Centre** 023 8089 2077 C PB S W. Curdridge: **Fairthorne Manor YMCA** 01489 785228 C K S. Farnborough: **Quayside Wake and Ski** Coleford Bridge Rd 01252 524375 Ri Wb WS. Fordingbridge: **New Forest Water Park** 01425 656868 JS Tu Wb WS. Portsmouth: **Portsmouth Outdoor Centre** 023 9266 3873 C PB S W. Riseley: **Wellington Country Park** 0118 932 6444 C S. Southampton: **Southampton Water Activity Centre** 023 8022 5525 C PB S W, **Woodmill Outdoor Centre** 023 8055 5993 C K RBd.
ISLE OF WIGHT: Freshwater: **West Wight Sports Centre** Moa Pl 01983 752168 C Sn. Newport: **Medina Valley Centre** Dodnor La 01983 522195 C S. Shanklin: **Wight Water Adventure Sports** 01983 866269 C K S Sf W. West Cowes: **Island Youth Water Activities Centre** Arctic Rd 01983 293073 C PB S, **UK Sailing Academy** 01983 294941 K S W. Wootton: **3D Education & Adventure** Little Canada Centre New Rd 01983 885400 C DB K S.

YOUTH HOSTELLING

Introduce children to Youth Hostels for years of enjoyable family holidays! There are over 200 Youth Hostels in England and Wales based in towns, cities, on the coast or in the countryside and most have family rooms. You can self-cater or be cooked for, stay for one night or as long as you like; youth hostelling offers flexibility and choice. New for 2004 is the 'Top Bunk Club', especially for children aged 5-12 years. To find out more visit www.yha.org.uk or call 0870 770 8868 and quote 'Let's Go 04'. For details of 25% off membership offer **check out page 40.**

Each choose a letter.
See how many objects you can spot, either in the car or out of the window, beginning with the letter in a given time.
Keep a list.

YHA - Bursting with ideas!

What are YOU doing this weekend? Call 0870 770 8868 and quote LETS GO 04 for your family pack and voucher for 25% off YHA membership.

www.yha.org.uk
Registered Charity No. 306122

The Face Place

Parties for girls

Make-overs Fabulous nails
Fantasy Faces
Funky hair styles
(choose your style and take home the accessories)
Fabulous Party Bags
Raffle included
Craft Corner too
Heaven for girls!
Tailor-made Party packages for all ages, for great times!

01202 419424
07736 684206

email: sys.tem@virgin.com
Visit our website at
www.thefaceplace.co.uk

AVON BEACH
MUDEFORD: CHRISTCHURCH
★★★★★

Family run business, 65 YEARS

Great Food
Café, shops and family Beach. For great food, comfortable Surroundings, friendly service. Full meal or just a cake and coffee. Open everyday (excluding Xmas day). Great gift ideas, books, novelties. Beach goods.

Great Place
A good family beach with a promenade for easy walking. Have fun in the water, hire a beach hut or a Canoe. Volley ball during the summer weeks. Parking right on the sea front, (charges apply).

Open everyday
Avon Beach Mudeford, Christchurch.
Tel: 01425 272162 Fax: 01425 272043

THE HAWTHORNS URBAN WILDLIFE CENTRE

Interactive displays
Hands-on Activity Room
Activity Days during school holidays (please ring for details)
Nature trails in the wildlife garden
Events progamme all year round
Gift shop
Disabled access
Free entrance

The Hawthorns Urban Wildlife Centre
The Common
Southampton
Tel: 023 8067 1921
www.southampton.gov.uk

Open
10am-5pm Monday-Friday
12noon-4pm Saturday and Sunday

Free Places

Included here are free places of interest in the area, also museums, parks, open spaces and other places that offer free family entertainment and some ideas of activities you can participate in.

Although free admission, there may be significant car parking charges, extra charges for schools and special activities or requests for donations.

Some of your days out to free places will be the most memorable if you plan ahead; go for a family picnic and bicycle ride and discover the free pleasures around locally.

DORSET

Abbotsbury, The Macmillan Way, 01789 740852. Coast to coast path that takes in beautiful countryside from Boston, Lincs to Abbotsbury. It also offers opportunities for fund raising to help this well-known cancer care charity. **Open all year.**

Ashley Heath, Moors Valley Country Park, Horton Road, www.moors-valley.co.uk 01425 470721. A play trail and tree-top walk built among the trees on Forestry Commission land with an adventure playground, nature trails, narrow-gauge railway and golf course (charge made) and a Go Ape! high ropes course. Park open daily, 8am-8pm or dusk if earlier. Steam railway, daily in Summer, Sat-Sun and school hols in Winter. Visitor centre open daily, from 9.30am. Schools Birthdays **Open all year.**

Bournemouth, Bournemouth Kids Free Fun Festival, The Pagoda, Lower Gardens, 01202 451713. During school Summer hols there is daily entertainment with clowns, magicians, puppet shows and wandering minstrels. On Wed nights the Candle Illuminations in the Lower Gardens feature 15,000 candles in coloured glass jars and at 10pm on a Fri, there is the Inshore Direct Firework Display from the Pier.
Fernheath Adventure Playground, Verney Road, 01202 581008. Open-access scheme for 5-14 year olds. Outdoor fun includes aerial runway, climbing frame and rope swing. Small indoor activity hut. Open Sat-Sun and school hols, 10am-1pm, 2-4.30pm. Closed Bank Hols.
Littledown Park, Chaseside, Castle Lane. In open parkland, surrounding the Sports Complex, are a large wildfowl lake, a children's play area, a paddling pool and adventure play equipment.
The Russell-Cotes Art Gallery and Museum, East Cliff, www.russell-cotes.bournemouth.gov.uk 01202 451858, is a Victorian cliff-top museum. The children's activity gallery offers creative opportunities and the family trail book encourages exploration through the museum. Open Tues-Sun, 10am-5pm. Schools **Open all year.**

Christchurch, Christchurch Priory, 01202 485804, is the longest parish church in England. Guided tours available. Open daily, Mon-Sat, 9.30am-5pm, Sun, 2.15-5.30pm. Donations. Schools **Open all year.**
Hengistbury Head, is a Nature Reserve and Site of Special Scientific Interest. A land train takes visitors to Mudeford Spit where there is a café and sandy beach. **Open all year.**

Dorchester(near), Maiden Castle, EH, off A354, is a spectacular Iron-Age hill fort. Display boards. Children will love to explore the maze of banks and ditches and imagine trying to defend the fort against Roman attack. Schools. **Open all year.**

Isle of Portland, Tout Quarry Sculpture Park and Nature Reserve, near Fortuneswell, 01305 820207. Discover sculptures carved into the rock face or worked from the quarry landscape. Paths take in spectacular sea views and the site is home to rare plants and butterflies. Schools **Open all year.**

Mudeford, Avon Beach, www.avon-beach.co.uk 01425 272162. Spend the day in a glorious setting with safe bathing, a café with sun terrace for meals, snacks and much more. Browse around the excellent gift and book shops. Also available are watersports, beach hut hire, BBQs and ice creams. **Check out page 40.**

Poole, Poole Park, 01202 261303. The park borders 55 acres of sea water and two fresh water lakes with swans, ducks and geese, and includes a children's playground. There is crazy golf, a putting green, miniature railway and Gus Gorilla's Jungle Playground and café. Check out `Adventure' chapter. **Open all year.**

RNLI Headquarters, West Quay Road, 01202 663000, has a small museum. All visits to the HQ and depot by prior appointment. Museum open Mon-Fri, 9am-5pm. Schools **Open all year.**

Scaplen's Court Museum, High Street, 01202 633558. A beautifully restored domestic building with recreations of a Victorian classroom and kitchen. Open to the public daily during Aug only, Mon-Sat, 10am-5pm, Sun, 12noon-5pm. Schools.

Upton Country Park, off A35, 01202 672625. The Upton House estate includes farmland, woodland and saltmarsh with nature trails and a replica Roman farm. Park open daily, 9am-dusk. Schools Birthdays **Open all year.**

Waterfront Museum, High Street, www.poole.gov.uk 01202 683138, gives a fascinating look into Poole's past including the discovery of an Iron-Age log-boat in the harbour and through its smuggling days. Open daily, Apr-Oct, 10am-5pm, Sun, 12noon-5pm, Nov-Mar, 10am-3pm, Sun, 12noon-3pm. Schools **Open all year.**

St Leonards, Avon Heath Country Park, Brocks Pine, 01425 478470. Explore 580 acres of heathland, home to rare and endangered plants and animals. Enjoy a walk or cycle along one of the trails. Events organised in hols. Park gates open Apr-Sept, 8am-7.30pm, Oct-Mar, 8.30am-5.30pm. Visitor centre open daily, 11am-4pm. Schools Birthdays **Open all year.**

Swanage, Durlston Country Park, Clifftop, 01929 424443. Woodland and wildlife trails can be followed across unspoilt countryside. The park centre has displays on marine life and cliff-nesting birds. Centre open daily, Apr-Oct, 10am-5pm, Winter, Sat-Sun, 10.30am-4pm. Schools **Open all year.**

Swanage Lifeboat Station, Peveril Point, to the east of town, www.swanagelifeboat.org.uk 01929 423237. View an Inshore D Class and an all-weather Mersey in the boathouse. Open Mon-Fri during daylight hours in Summer. Phone for Winter opening. Schools.

Toller Porcorum, Kingcombe Meadows Nature Reserve, 01305 264620, managed by the Dorset Wildlife Trust, has a network of footpaths across the area, famous for its patchwork of fields, woodland, scrub and bog. Visitor centre open daily, 8am-5pm. Schools **Open all year.**

West Lulworth, Lulworth Heritage Centre, 01929 400587. World famous for its geological features, visit the Lulworth Rock, Smuggling and Iron-Age exhibitions. Centre open daily, Mar-Oct, 10am-5pm, Nov-Feb, 4pm. Schools **Open all year.**

Weymouth, Brewers Quay, Hope Square, www.brewers-quay.co.uk 01305 777622, is an unusual leisure and shopping complex and includes 'Timewalk' and 'Discovery'. Check out `History' chapter. Numerous special events. Open daily, 10am-5.30pm, closed last two weeks of Jan. **Open all year.**

Radipole Lake RSPB Nature Reserve, 01305 778313. Paths lead through the reed beds around the freshwater lake where many different birds can be seen. The visitor centre has large viewing windows and there is a programme of walks and events, including children's trails. Centre open daily, 9am-5pm, Nov-Feb, 4pm. Schools **Open all year.**

Weymouth Beach, traditional Punch & Judy, swingboats, trampolining and more.

HAMPSHIRE

The New Forest, offers a rich variety of landscapes free to enjoy – woodland, open heathland and acres of space for picnics and games. There are waymarked trails at Blackwater and Bolderwood.

Aldershot, Brickfields Country Park, Boxalls Lane, 01252 330966. Opportunities here for a variety of nature studies. **Open all year.**
Rowhill Nature Reserve, Cranmore Lane, off A325, 01252 319749, is a 55-acre site, mostly wooded with ponds, streams, heathland, a large meadow and field centre. Centre open Sun, 2-4.30pm. Schools **Open all year.**

Aldershot and Farnborough, Rushmoor Events, 01252 398000. Victoria Day Fayre in July, 01252 323232. Green Family Fun Day and Flower Festival in July, 01252 398000. Rushmoor Fireworks Spectacular, Manor Park first Sat in Nov.

Alton, The Curtis Museum and Allen Gallery, High Street, 01420 82802. The museum depicts local history from the Ice Age to the present day and houses a ceramics collection. The gallery (in Church Street) has exhibitions and a garden. Open Tues-Sat, 10am-5pm. Schools **Open all year.**

Andover, Andover Museum, 6 Church Close, 01264 366283, traces Andover's history from Saxons to present day. Special exhibitions in the gallery and an aquarium showing fish found in the River Test. Open Tues-Sat, 10am-5pm. Schools **Open all year.**
Museum of the Iron Age, 6 Church Close, 01264 366283, adjoining Andover Museum, includes information and displays from the excavations at the nearby Danebury Ring Iron-Age Hill Fort. Open Mon-Sat, 10am-5pm, Easter-Sept, Sun and Bank Hol Mons, 2-5pm. Schools **Open all year.**

Basingstoke, Willis Museum, Old Town Hall, Market Place, 01256 465902, has a programme of visiting exhibitions and a gallery 'Basingstoke through 200 years'. Quiz sheets available. Open Mon-Fri, 10am-5pm, Sat, 10am-4pm. Schools **Open all year.**

Bursledon, Manor Farm Country Park, Jn 8 M27, 01489 787055. Enjoy the countryside and wildlife of the upper reaches of the Hamble River. Children's play areas, space for ball games and picnic areas. Car parking charge. Check out `Farms'. Schools **Open all year.**

Eastleigh, Eastleigh Museum and Art Gallery, 25 High Street, 023 8064 3026. Museum is very small, covering local history with changing exhibitions every six weeks. Open Tues-Fri, 10am-5pm, Sat, 10am-4pm. Schools **Open all year.**
Fleming Park Recreation Ground, 023 8068 4800, has an outdoor children's play area and paddling pool. Tennis courts, football and cricket pitches must be booked. **Open all year.**

Eastleigh(near), Lakeside Country Park, off the A335 Eastleigh-Southampton Road, 023 8061 7882. A popular waterpark with open grassland and day fishing by permit. The lakes can be booked for watersport activities. A miniature railway runs every weekend and daily during school hols. Schools **Open all year.**

Fareham, The Royal Armouries Museum, Fort Nelson, Down End Road, www.armouries.org.uk 01329 233734. A restored Victorian artillery fort overlooking Portsmouth Harbour. It houses the national collection of artillery, spanning centuries of British and world history. Open Apr-Oct, 10am-5pm, Nov-Mar, 10.30am-4pm. Phone for details of special events. Schools **Open all year.**
Westbury Manor Museum, 84 West Street, 01329 824895, houses exciting displays on all aspects of the area's local and natural history. Open Mon-Fri, 10am-5pm, Sat, 10am-4pm. Closed some Bank Hols. Schools **Open all year.**

Farnborough, Farnborough Air Sciences Museum, Trenchard House, Farnborough Road, www.FASTA.co.uk 01252 375050. See wind tunnels where vital wartime research took place and the transonic tunnel in which the aerodynamics of high speed flight were investigated, resulting in the success of Concorde. Suitable for older children. Open Sat-Sun, 10am-4pm. Donations welcome. Schools.

Fordingbridge, Hockeys Farm, South Gorley, 01425 652542, is a conservation farm with a deer park and bird sanctuary. There is a children's play area and a farm shop. Open Tues-Sat, 8am-5pm. **Open all year.**

Gosport, Gosport Museum, Walpole Road, 023 9258 8035, has a local history gallery, geology gallery 'The Gosport Time Machine', art gallery and coffee shop. Open Tues-Sat, 10am-5pm. Schools **Open all year.**

Havant, Havant Museum, East Street, 023 9245 1155. Discover the link between Havant and the Treaty of Versailles and the area's history and development. A Clock Gallery is the latest addition. Open Tues-Sat, 10am-5pm. Schools **Open all year.**

Horndean, Queen Elizabeth Country Park, 023 9259 5040, offers extensive trails for walking, horse riding, orienteering and off-road cycling and a children's adventure play trail. Visitor centre open daily, Apr-Oct, 10am-5.30pm, Nov-Dec, 10am-4.30pm or dusk, Jan-Mar, Sat-Sun only, 10am-5.30pm or dusk. Schools **Open all year.**

Lepe, Lepe Country Park, 023 8089 9108. Most of the park is an attractive coastal strip with beaches, picnic areas and walks. There is a children's play area near the information centre. Park open daily. Phone for centre opening times. Schools **Open all year.**

Lyndhurst(near), The New Forest Reptile Centre, Holidays Hill, off A35, 023 8028 3141. A rare chance to see all the reptiles and amphibians of the New Forest, including adders, grass snakes, smooth snakes, lizards, frogs and toads. Self-guided trails and ranger guides available. Open daily, Easter-Sept, 10am-4pm. Schools.

Netley, Royal Victoria Country Park, 023 8045 5157, has 230 acres of woodland and parkland for walks, picnics and a seashore for beachcombing. A miniature steam railway operates during the school hols and weekends, and there are children's play areas. Check out `History' chapter. Schools **Open all year.**

Petersfield, The Bear Museum, 38 Dragon St, 01730 265108. The world's oldest bear museum has small rooms crammed with a teddy collection. No wheeled access. Open Tues-Sat, 10am-4.30pm. **Open all year.**

Portsmouth, Portsmouth City Museum and Records Office, Museum Road, 023 9282 7261, has displays covering the development of Portsmouth from the Ice Age to the 1950s. Craft activity programmes are available for schools and during weekends and school hols for family groups. Open daily, Apr-Sept, 10am-5.30pm, Oct-Mar, 5pm. Schools **Open all year.**

Sherfield on Loddon, Longbridge Mill, 01256 883483, is an 800-year-old large working water mill with a visitor centre. Milling demonstrations take place on the fourth Sat of each month between 12noon-4pm. Open to view daily during restaurant hours, 11.30am-10pm. Schools **Open all year.**

Southampton, City Walls, 023 8086 8401. Sections of the walls remain around the old town, some connected by a special walk starting at Bargate, with information panels. **Open all year.**
Hawthorns Urban Wildlife Centre, The Common, 023 8067 1921, offers facilities that include an Activities Room with interactive games and activities, a Display Room with living examples of some of the smaller creatures found in and around Southampton's open spaces, and a large garden developed to show a diversity of habitats demonstrating the wide range of flora

and fauna in the Southampton area. Schools are very welcome. The staff are knowledgeable and an enthusiastic Education Officer will tailor a visit to complement classroom activities as well as programmes of study as required by the National Curriculum. Please telephone for details of children's activities during school holidays. Open daily, Mon-Fri, 10am-5pm, Sat-Sun, 12noon-4pm. (Closed Bank Hols.) **Schools Open all year Check out page 40.**

Southampton City Art Gallery, North Guild, 023 8083 2277, is one of the finest in the country. Open Tues-Sat, 10am-5pm, Sun, 1-4pm. **Schools Open all year.**

Southampton Museums, 023 8063 5904. The following two museums cover maritime heritage and archaeology. Events, workshops and worksheets are provided. Open Tues-Sun. Phone for opening times. **Schools Open all year.**

The Maritime Museum, The Wool House, Town Quay Road, has a huge model of Southampton Docks and many models of ships. Look out for the Queen Mary and the exhibition of the Titanic disaster.

Museum of Archaeology, God's House Tower, Winkle Street, has exhibitions on Roman, Saxon and medieval Southampton, housed in part of the old city walls. Object Activity room for children.

SS Shieldhall, Berth 48, Southampton Docks, 023 8023 0405, is the last fully working cargo and passenger steamship to explore. Call for details of the occasional public sailings in the Solent during the Summer and for opening times. Donations welcome. **Schools.**

Stockbridge(near), Danebury Ring, 01962 860948, is one of the finest Iron-Age hill forts in southern Britain and also a Site of Special Scientific Interest for flora. Check out the Museum of the Iron Age, Andover, in `History' chapter. **Schools Open all year.**

Totton, Totton and Eling Heritage Centre, 122 Eling Lane, 023 8066 6339. Local history depicted through information panels and three-dimensional scenes (including smells!). Temporary exhibition area, resources room for local family and history research and café. Open Easter-Oct, Wed-Sun, 10am-4pm, Nov-Easter, 10.30am-4pm. **Schools Open all year.**

West End, Itchen Valley Country Park, Allington Lane, 023 8046 6091, is a large area of unspoilt countryside with waymarked trails through woodland and meadows, picnic sites (with BBQ hire) and a large adventure play area. High Wood Barn Visitor Centre has interpretive displays, information and audio-visual programmes about the park, a shop and café. A varied programme of countryside activities offers something for all the family, from guided walks to playschemes, pond dipping to treasure hunts. New for 2004 is an animal play sculpture trail. Park open daily, Visitor Centre, Apr-Sept, daily, 11am-5.30pm, Oct-Mar, Sat, Sun & school hols, 11am-4.30pm. **Schools Open all year Check out page 47.**

Winchester, City Museum, The Square, 01962 848269, tells the story of Winchester from prehistoric and Roman past to the present day. Open Apr-Oct, Mon-Sat, 10am-5pm, Sun, 12noon-5pm; Nov-Mar, Tues-Sat, 10am-4pm, Sun, 12noon-4pm. **Schools.**

The Great Hall, Castle Avenue, High Street, 01962 846476, was built in the early 13th century, as part of the original medieval castle. It houses the famous King Arthur Round Table. Open daily, 10am-5pm. **Schools Open all year.**

The King's Royal Hussars Museum, Peninsula Barracks, Romsey Road, 01962 828541. The history of three famous Cavalry Regiments, including the Charge of the Light Brigade, is told here. Open Tues-Fri, 10am-1pm, 1.30-4pm, weekends and Mons, 12noon-4pm. **Schools Open all year.**

The Light Infantry Museum, Peninsula Barracks, Romsey Road, 01962 828550. The story of a modern regiment, including the Fall of the Berlin Wall and Gulf War. Open Tues-Sat, 10am-12.30pm, 1.30-4pm, Sun, 12noon-4pm. Open Mons during school hols. **Schools Open all year.**

Royal Hampshire Regiment Museum, Southgate Street, 01962 863658, covers the history of the Regiment from 1702. Reopening in May 2004 after refurbishment. Open Apr-Oct, Mon-Fri, 11am-3.30pm, Sat, Sun and Bank Hols, 12noon-4pm. **Schools.**

Free Places

The Westgate Museum, High Street, 01962 869864. Fortified medieval gateway, once a debtors' prison, with examples of 17th-century graffiti! Good selection of brass rubbings (small charge). Open Apr-Oct, Mon-Sat, 10am-5pm, Sun, 12noon-5pm, Feb-Mar, Tues-Sun, 10am-4pm. Schools.

Winchester Cathedral, 01962 857200. Built for William the Conqueror, the architecture is Norman with Gothic overlay and Jane Austen is buried here. Children's workshops, trails and tours are available. Education centre open Mon-Fri, 8am-4.30pm. Donations expected. Schools **Open all year.**

TRAVEL GAMES

Each choose a colour. Count how many vehicles of your chosen colour you see in a given time. Or the first one to reach ten.

Variations - This can also be played by choosing a number. Score 1 point for each number seen on a plate. If the number is repeated once on the same plate score 5 points and if 3 occur score 10 points. Either play with a time limit or the first to reach 20.

SALISBURY AREA

Salisbury, Churchill Gardens, Southampton Road. A formal park with a lovely riverside walk. There is also a skatepark, roller hockey pitch and a fenced area with play equipment for younger children. **Open all year.**

Queen Elizabeth Gardens, Crane Bridge Road. Overlooking the Cathedral and water meadows, this attractive park has a good, fenced children's play area. **Open all year.**

Salisbury Cathedral, www.salisburycathedral.org.uk 01722 555120, is a medieval masterpiece. See an original Magna Carta, follow the children's trail looking for animals and symbols or take a guided tower tour (age/height restrictions apply). Donations expected. Open daily, 7.15am-6.15pm; special events restrict access. Schools **Open all year.**

ISLE OF WIGHT

Enjoy the many beaches of the island including the quieter Whitecliff, Seaview, Bembridge, Colwell Bay, Compton and Totland Bay and look out for the safe 'KidZones'. Take the family walking or cycling on dedicated trails. Cycle route leaflet available from the Tourist Office, 01983 813818.

The National Trust looks after Tennyson Down, Headon Warren and Compton Bay in the West, Ventnor Downs and St Catherine's Hill in the South, Borthwood Copse, Priory Wood and Bembridge Downs in the East. For more information phone 01983 741020. **Check out page 22.**

Arreton, Arreton Old Village and Barns, 01983 528353. Woodturning, glass blowing and jewellery-making can be viewed and children can take part in clay modelling. Brass rubbing centre. Schools **Open all year.**

Brighstone, Brighstone Museum, NT, North Street, 01983 740689, contains mementoes from the history of the village. Open Apr-Dec, Mon-Sat, 10am-5pm, Sun, 12noon-5pm, Jan-Mar, 10am-1pm. **Schools Open all year.**

Cowes, Maritime Museum, Cowes Library, Beckford Road, 01983 293341, is tiny and features models, paintings and photographs of the maritime history of the island. Open Mon-Wed, Fri, 9.30am-6pm, Sat, 9.30am-4.30pm. **Schools Open all year.**

Godshill, The Old Smithy and Gardens, www.theoldsmithy.com 01983 840364. See models of places of interest, an aviary, herb garden and café. Open daily, 10am-5.30pm. **Schools Open all year.**

Ryde, Appley Park, is a large fenced play area with a pitch and putt and a marked cycle route from Appley Park to Seaview.

Sandown, Glory Art Glass, Melville Street, www.gloryartglass.com 01983 402515. Demonstrations of glass blowing are held during Apr-Oct at 11am and 4.30pm. Shop and display rooms open Mon-Sat, 9.30am-5pm. **Schools Open all year.**

Ventnor, Ventnor Botanic Garden, Undercliff Drive, www.botanic.co.uk 01983 855397. Find many rare and exotic plants, enjoy the fenced play area and pop in to the visitors centre. Open daily, 10am-5pm, Nov-Mar, Sat-Sun only, 10am-4pm. **Schools Open all year.**

Wroxall, Isle of Wight Donkey Sanctuary, Lower Winstone Farm, www.donksanc.demon.co.uk 01983 852693, is a permanent home to over 200 rescued donkeys and many other animals. Open Easter-Sept, 10.30am-4.30pm. Donations welcomed. **Schools.**

Yarmouth(near), Fort Victoria Country Park, www.fortvictoria.co.uk 01983 823893, offers seashore and woodland walks and ranger-led guided walks. Vantage points for watching the Solent's boats and shipping. **Schools Open all year.**

Free Places

Choose a topic from this list:

**GIRLS NAMES
BOYS NAMES
MUSICAL INSTRUMENTS
ARTICLES OF CLOTHING
ANIMALS
FRUITS OR VEGETABLES
TREES OR PLANTS
PARTS OF A CAR**

One person starts by naming one thing in the category, such as Girls Names eg RACHEL
The next person has to call out another name, not yet used, beginning with the last letter of the previous word, eg LAURA, the next person could say ANNE, and so on.

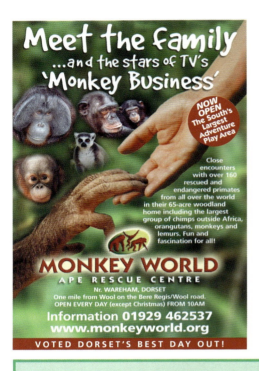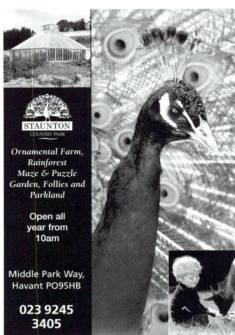

Farms, Wildlife & Nature Parks

All children love animals and sea life and there are many species to be found within this area, either in farm surroundings, animal parks or sea life parks. Enjoy also a range of nature parks and gardens. Places listed here have admission charges, but there are places of natural interest which are free to visit. Check out 'Free Places' as well, so you don't miss anything.

DORSET

Abbotsbury, Abbotsbury Swannery, New Barn Road, www.abbotsbury-tourism.co.uk 01305 871130. Watch the family life of swans in this free-flying colony. Guided tours for booked parties. Baby swans hatching May-end Jun. Daily mass feeding at 12noon and 4pm. Open daily, 20th Mar-3rd Oct, 10am-6pm, 4th Oct-31st Oct, 5pm. Under 5s free. Schools Price C.

Children's Farm and Smugglers Barn, 01305 871130. Outdoor and indoor fun for under 11s. Meet rabbits, guinea pigs, ponies and donkeys in this rural setting. Bottle-feed baby goats and milk Molly the magic cow or just let off steam in the ancient Barn play area. Open daily, 20th Mar-3rd Oct, 10am-6pm, 4th Oct-23rd Oct, Sat-Sun only, 10am-5pm. Schools Price B.

Sub Tropical Gardens, 01305 871130. A 20-acre garden with Jubilee Sculpture Trail, golden pheasants, owls and kookaburras, ponds and streams. Children's play area and colonial-style tea house. Open daily, Easter-Oct, 10am-6pm, Nov-Mar, 10am-4pm. Schools Open all year Price C (passport ticket for all three venues Price D).

Beaminster, UK Llamas, Mosterton, www.ukllamas.co.uk 01308 868674. Learn about llamas with a hands-on introduction or go for a short llama trek. Phone for details and prices. Schools Birthdays Open all year.

Bournemouth, The Oceanarium, Seafront, www.oceanarium.co.uk 01202 311993, brings you face-to-face with marine life from around the globe. An interactive experience with touch-screen games, feeding demonstrations, plasma-screen documentaries, walk-through underwater tunnel and exhibits. Café and gift shop. Open daily, 10am-5pm. Schools Open all year Price B.

Brownsea Island, Brownsea Island, NT, 01202 707744. A beautiful 500-acre island of heath and woodland with miles of woodland walks and open glades. The red squirrel survives here. Coffee shop. Open daily, 27th Mar-23rd Jul, 10am-5pm, 24th Jul-31st Aug, 10am-6pm, 1st Sept-31st Oct, 10am-5pm. Check time of last boat. Boats from Poole Quay and Sandbanks. Schools Price A.

Buckland Newton, Badger and Wildlife Watch, Old Henley Farm, Dorchester, www.badgerwatchdorset.co.uk 01300 345293. A rare treat! Watch the night-time activities of wildlife from a purpose-built hide. Stay for an hour or until dawn. Early booking essential. Schools Open all year Price D.

Charmouth, Charmouth Heritage Coast Centre, Seafront, www.charmouth.org 01297 560772. Join the wardens here for a guided fossil hunt or Seashore Safari. Watch the short film in the Jurassic Theatre for inspiration! A must for fossil hunters and rock poolers. Admission to the centre free. Open daily, 10.30am-5pm, Easter-Oct half-term. Schools Price B.

Dorchester, Kingston Maurward Gardens, www.kmc.ac.uk 01305 215003. Enjoy 35 acres of exquisite gardens. The Animal Park has an interesting collection of unusual breeds of animals which children can sometimes help to feed. Open daily, 10am-5.30pm or dusk. Schools Open all year Price B.

Furzebrook, The Blue Pool, 01929 551408. Sandy paths meander through 25 acres of heather, gorse and pine trees up to views of the Purbeck Hills or down steps to the magical Blue Pool. There is a small play area and museum. Grounds open Easter-Nov, 9.30am-5.30pm, tea house and shops, 10am-5pm. Schools Price A.

Langton Matravers, Putlake Adventure Farm, 01929 422917. Meet a variety of farm animals, bottle feed lambs, try hand milking, follow the farmland trail, or picnic by the duck pond. Open daily, Feb half-term, Apr-Oct, 11am-6pm, Nov-Dec, Feb-Mar, Sat-Sun only. Schools Birthdays Price B.

Lyme Regis, Lyme Regis Marine Aquarium and Cobb History, The Cobb, 01297 33106. Discover the variety of local sea life in a long 'look over' viewing tank and smaller eye-level tanks. New for 2004 Ocean Awareness Centre. Learn about fishing, rigs, tides and the ocean. Group talks by arrangement. Open daily, Mar-Nov, 10am-5pm (7pm in high season). Schools Price A.

Poole, Compton Acres, Canford Cliffs, www.comptonacres.co.uk 01202 700110. Individually themed gardens that include the Italian garden and Canadian woodland walk with interactive games. Home to a family of muntjac deer, see them being fed at regular feeding times. Visit the scenic model railway. Children's quiz cards available. Open daily, 9am-6pm. Schools Birthdays Open all year Price B.

Farmer Palmer's Farm Park, Organford, 01202 622022. A diversified dairy farm with all the fun of a children's farm. Supervised feeding of lambs and handling of guinea pigs. Let off steam on Straw Mountain or in the undercover play area. Open daily, Apr-Sept, 10am-5.30pm, Winter opening, weekends and half-term hols, 10am-4pm. Birthdays Price B.

Sherborne, Worldlife and the Lullingstone Silk Farm, off A30, www.wwb.co.uk 01935 474608. Learn about butterflies, moths, stick insects and silk in a beautiful parkland location. New for 2004 a tropical house with exotic plants and over 200 butterflies. Open daily, Apr-Sept, 10am-5pm. Schools Price B.

Stapehill, Stapehill Abbey, Crafts, Gardens and Museum, E of Wimborne on old A31, 01202 861686. See crafts people at work in a garden setting. The 'Power to the Land' exhibition shows how mechanical power has changed rural life. Farmyard animals, playground and picnic area. Open daily, Easter-Sept, 10am-5pm; Oct-Dec and Feb-Easter, Wed-Sun, 10am-4pm. Schools Price B.

Toller Porcorum, The Kingcombe Centre, 01300 320684, offers day and residential courses studying the countryside. Children's holiday activities include painting, wildlife exploring, and exploring life in fresh water. Charges vary. Schools Open all year.

Wareham, Monkey World, Ape Rescue Centre, one mile N of Wool, on the Bere Regis road, www.monkeyworld.org 01929 462537. This internationally acclaimed ape rescue centre is home to over 160 primates rescued from all over the world including the largest group of chimpanzees outside Africa. Children can go bananas in the biggest adventure play area on the south coast and half-hourly Keepers' Talks reveal the stories of the primate stars of TV's 'Monkey Business' programme. A woodland walk, pets corner, soft play area, education centre, café, picnic areas and gift shop ensure that Monkey World is a great day out for all. Open daily, 10am-5pm. (Jul-Aug, 6pm). Schools Birthdays Open all year Price C Check out page 48.

Weymouth, Weymouth Sea Life Park, Lodmoor Country Park, 01305 761070. Discover fascinating sea creatures in an underwater world. Have fun in the classroom of the Shark Academy or visit the lair of the octopus. Seal, otter and penguin sanctuaries. Open daily, 10am-5pm. Check out `Adventure' chapter. Schools Birthdays Open all year Price C.

Wimborne(near), Honeybrook Farm, on B3078, 01202 881120, is a restored country farm and park. Country life as it was, with hand milking and animal feeding. Visitors can enjoy a heavy horse cart or pony ride. Don't miss Pets Corner, the adventure play area, tearooms and farm shop. Phone for opening details. Schools Price B.

HAMPSHIRE

Ampfield, Sir Harold Hillier Gardens, Jermyns Lane, near Romsey, www.hilliergardens.org.uk 01794 368787. Enjoy the 180-acre public garden with themed landscapes and a multitude of plants. See the new Visitor & Education Pavilion. Pre-school activities and Tots and Tinies every two weeks, children's activities during school hols. Open daily, 10.30am-6pm or dusk. Under 16s free. Schools Open all year Price B.

Andover, Finkley Down Farm Park, www.finkleydownfarm.co.uk 01264 352195, on the outskirts of the town, is well signposted off the major roads. It is a splendid place to take children, especially under 10s, for a friendly taste of natural farm life and to introduce them at close hand to the farm pig or calf. In a very relaxed environment there is a lot to see and do and much to learn with a great variety of tame, young animals for children to stroke and feed, including rabbits and lambs. You might even be lucky enough to see newly hatched chicks or ducklings. There are activities throughout the day, such as Rabbit Handling, Pony Grooming and Egg Collecting. A countryside museum contains interesting bygones and a Romany encampment. Children will enjoy the marvellous adventure playground which is close to a large picnic area. There is also a gift shop and tea room. Open daily, 14th Mar-31st Oct, 10am-6pm. Schools Birthdays Price B Check out page 48.

Ashurst, The New Forest Otter, Owl and Wildlife Conservation Park, Longdown, www.ottersandowls.co.uk Tel: 023 8029 2408. Set in 25 acres of ancient woodland in the New Forest, the Park cares for a collection of multi-specied otters, owls and other indigenous wildlife including birds of prey. Follow the circular nature trail to experience at close proximity and in near natural surroundings the world of Asian short-claw otters, lynx, badgers, pine martens, field mice, deer, wallabies and wild boar and many other creatures. Look out for special talks and feeding times. A major focus of the Park is to rehabilitate injured species into the wild and there is an on-going breeding programme for all otters and owls. Hot and cold refreshments available, with a picnic area close by. Open daily, 10am-6pm, weekends only in Jan. Schools Open all year Price B Check out page 54.

Ashurst(near), Longdown Activity Farm, www.longdownfarm.co.uk 023 8029 3326, offers fun for all the family whatever the weather, with a variety of hands-on activities every day. These include small animal handling, bottle-feeding goat kids and calves, pony grooming and tractor and trailer rides. There are indoor and outdoor play areas, with trampolines and ball pools, Land Rover driving for adults and pedal tractors for children. Watch the afternoon milking from the viewing gallery. Free guided tour for school groups. If you visit Santa's Grotto during December, there's a gift for every child. Tearoom, picnic areas and gift shop. Open daily, 14th Feb-Dec (please ring to confirm), 10am-5pm. Schools Birthdays Price B Check out page 54.

Beaulieu(near), Exbury Gardens, Info Lines 023 8089 9422/023 8089 1203. Explore the fine woodland gardens, follow the seasonal trails to the home of the 'Queen of the Fairies' and ride on the miniature steam railway. Santa Steam Specials at Christmas. Take a picnic or relax in the tearoom. Open daily, Mar-Nov, 10am-5.30pm or dusk. Under 10s free. Schools Price A/B.

Bursledon, Manor Farm, inside the Country Park, Jn 8 M27, 01489 787055. Visit a working Hampshire farm and farmhouse of a bygone age. There are special events and demonstrations throughout the year. Open daily, Easter-Oct, 10am-5pm, Nov-Easter, Sun only and Feb half-term, 10am-4pm. (Country Park open all year.) Schools Birthdays Open all year Price B.

Farms, Wildlife & Nature Parks

Colden Common, Marwell Zoological Park, off the Bishops Waltham to Winchester road, www.marwell.org.uk (email: marwell@marwell.org.uk) 07626 943163, provides the only opportunity in Hampshire to see snow leopards, rhinos, tigers and many other wild and endangered animals. The zoo has succeeded in returning some endangered species to their natural habitat in the wild and young animals can be seen all year round. Enjoy your visit by walking the well-planned route amongst the spacious enclosures. Take a ride on the 15" gauge railway or let the free road train give you a different view of the zoo. Experience the rain forest in the Tropical House and don't miss Penguin World with its underwater viewing gallery. There are roundabouts, children's amusements and a big adventure playground with many picnic areas. Look out for the many special events organised during the year. Schools are welcome to use the excellent Education Service. Open daily, 10am-4pm (6pm in Summer). Schools Birthdays **Open all year Price D Check out page 52.**

Fareham, Haven House Visitor Centre and Titchfield Haven National Nature Reserve, Cliff Road Hill Head, 01329 662145. The centre provides information about the natural history of the Solent area. Special Events from bird watching to beach combing. Open Wed-Sun and Bank Hol Mons, 9.30am-5pm, 4pm Winter. Schools **Open all year Price A.**

Farnham, Birdworld and Underwater World, Holt Pound, www.birdworld.co.uk 01420 22140, in lovely landscaped grounds off the A325, is well worth a visit to see beautiful birds from all over the world, farm animals, exotic fish, creepy crawlies and more. Wander around the aviaries and themed areas to see a rich variety of shapes, sizes and colours. Be sure to see the amazing Toucan beak and find out how Hornbills nurture their young. Meet some friendly birds in the Heron Theatre and find out how an owl can fly silently when a pigeon makes so much noise. Join the Birds of Prey tour, watch the penguins feeding and visit Jenny Wren's Farm for an Animal Encounter (weather permitting). Don't miss the special event days and activity weeks throughout the year, particularly in school holidays. The enthusiastic Education Team ensure you have great fun learning from all the information and activity here. There are play areas and refreshment points throughout the Park. Birthday parties are available and school parties are welcome to make use of excellent educational material. There is also an Outreach team able to visit schools. The restaurant and shop can be visited without entering the Park. Fully open daily, 10am-6pm (4.30pm in Winter) from Feb half term-end Oct, all Winter school holiday periods and weekends from Nov-Feb half term. Birdworld gardens only, open at a reduced rate, weekdays in Winter outside school hols. Combined entrance ticket to Birdworld and Underwater World and an excellent Membership scheme is available for regular visitors. Schools Birthdays **Open all year Price D Check out inside back cover.**

Havant, Staunton Country Park, just off B2149 Petersfield Road, 023 9245 3405. A unique and enjoyable day out for all ages. Children will love the maze and Puzzle Garden and many different animals on the ornamental farm, including llamas and Shetlands. A children's paddock provides close contact with the animals and feed is available on entry. Enjoy a rainforest experience in the tropical glasshouses and explore follies in 1,000 acres of beautiful parkland with lakes, woods and well-marked trails. Take the time to appreciate the Victorian walled garden and new Sensory Garden. There is a new children's play area and shop. Refurbished farm area and tea rooms open Spring 2004. School parties welcome. Phone for details of special events throughout the year. Open daily, 10am-5pm (4pm Winter). Schools Birthdays **Open all year Price B Check out page 48.**

Headley, Children's Action Farm, near Newbury, www.actionfarm.com 01635 269666, has all-weather fun for the family. See the animals in the open and under cover and in the Animal Theatre. Enjoy a pony ride and let off steam in the Bouncy Castle and Adventure Play Ground. Café and soft play area. Open daily, 10am-5pm. Schools Birthdays **Open all year Price B/C.**

Riseley, Wellington Country Park, near Reading, www.wellington-country-park.co.uk 0118 9326444. Here are 350 acres of natural parkland on the Duke of Wellington's estate, making an

ideal venue for a family outing. Enjoy the nature trails and 35-acre lake with boats for hire and coarse fishing. Children will love the adventure playground, children's animal farm, miniature railway, crazy golf and sandpit. There is BBQ hire for family and other groups and a camping and caravan site (dogs welcome). Season tickets are now available. Open daily, 13th Mar-6th Nov, 10am-5.30pm. Please telephone for details of Winter weekend openings and special events. Schools Birthdays Price B Check out page 54.

Southsea, Blue Reef Aquarium, Clarence Esplanade, www.bluereefaquarium.co.uk 023 9287 5222. Enjoy an undersea safari as you view the variety of marine life from around the Solent coastline and see a coral reef and otter holt. A combination of sight, sound and smells makes for an unforgettable visit. Open daily, 10am-6pm Summer, Winter 5pm. Schools Birthdays Open all year Price B.

Weyhill, The Hawk Conservancy, just off the A303, www.hawk-conservancy.org 01264 772251. Watch birds of prey in flight, weather permitting, and hold one after flying demonstrations. Seven acres of wildflower meadows, an education centre, art gallery and play area. Children must be accompanied. No dogs or pets. Open daily, 14th Feb-31st Oct, 10.30am-5.30pm. Schools Birthdays Price C.

SALISBURY AREA

Cholderton, Cholderton Rare Breeds Farm Park, just off A303 between Amesbury and Andover, www.rabbitworld.co.uk 01980 629438. A wonderful variety of attractions. Touch and feed the animals or even take one for a walk. Visit Rabbit World to see over 50 different breeds or explore the replica Iron Age roundhouse farm. There are indoor and outdoor play and picnic areas, a nature trail, shop and tea-room, archaeology days for children and even a dig in August. YHA bunkhouse accommodation is now available on site. Open daily, 20th Mar-31st Oct, 10am-6pm; Winter, Sat-Sun, 11am-4pm, & at any time for groups by arrangement. Schools Birthdays Open all year Price B Check out page 57.

Teffont, Farmer Giles Farmstead, www.farmergiles.co.uk 01722 716338. Watch the cows being milked and bottle or hand-feed different animals on this working farm. Indoor and outdoor play areas. Open Mar-beg Nov, daily, 10am-5pm; Winter, Sat-Sun, and daily in school hols. Schools Birthdays Open all year Price B.

Tollard Royal, Larmer Tree Gardens, Rushmore Estate, www.larmertreegardens.co.uk 01725 516228. These grounds have ornamental birds, an adventure playground and an exhibition of colonial and oriental buildings with a children's trail. Open Apr-Jun and Aug-Oct, Sun-Thurs, 11am-4pm. Price B.

ISLE OF WIGHT

Binstead, Brickfields Horse Country, Newnham Road, near Ryde, www.brickfields.net 01983 566801. See giant shire horses and Shetland ponies and enjoy Parades, Donkeytown and Farm Corner. Open daily, 10am-5pm. Schools Birthdays Open all year Price B.

Brighstone(near), Dinosaur Farm Museum, Military Road, www.dinosaurfarm.co.uk 01983 740844. Unique dinosaur remains found on site and a life-sized reconstruction. Bring fossils for identification or enjoy a fossil hunt. Open Apr-Oct, Tues, Thurs, Sun, (daily, Jul-Aug), 10am-5pm. Schools Price A.

Mottistone, Mottistone Manor Garden, NT, 01983 741 302, is noted for its colourful herbaceous borders, grassy terraces and sea views. There is also a special quiz trail for children. Open 30th Mar-27th Oct, 11am-5.30pm, Tue-Wed, 28th Mar-31st Oct, 2-5.30pm, Sun only. Price A Check out page 22.

Farms, Wildlife & Nature Parks

Newchurch, Amazon World Zoo Park, Watery Lane, on the A3056, www.amazonworld.co.uk 01983 867122. Follow the story of the rainforest and discover diverse habitats of exotic creatures. Falconry Displays and 'Meet the Animals' talks. Open daily, 10am-5.30pm. Schools Birthdays **Open all year** Price B.

Porchfield, Colemans Animal Farm, Colemans Lane, 01983 522831. Meet lots of friendly farm animals and go wild in the Straw Fun barns. Open Easter-Oct, Tues-Sun, 10am–5pm. Schools Birthdays Price B.

Sandown(near), Branstone Farm Studies Centre, on the A3056, www.iwight.com/branstonefarm 01983 865540, is for schools and groups only. Learn about animal husbandry, farm techniques, conservation issues, interact with the animals and view cows being milked. Schools **Open all year.**

Seaview, Flamingo Park Wildlife Encounter, on the B330, www.flamingoparkiw.com 01983 612261. See over 100 flamingos and help feed koi carp, penguins, macaws and other birds. Visit Beaver Island and Pelican Bay. Open 29th Mar-31st Oct, 10am-5pm. Schools Birthdays Price C.

Shanklin, Shanklin Chine, 01983 866432, of special geological interest. Walk down to the shore beside waterfalls and visit the heritage centre. Open daily, 1st Apr-20th May, 27th Sept-31st Oct, 10am-5pm; 21st May-26th Sept, closes 10pm. Opening subject to weather conditions. Schools Price A.

Wootton, Butterfly World and Fountain World, Medina Garden Centre, Staplers Road, 01983 883430. See free-flying butterflies inside a tropical garden and an insectarium. Hand-feeding of fish daily, 11am, 2pm and 3.30pm. Open Apr-Oct, 10am-5pm. Schools Price B.

Wroxall, Owl and Falconry Centre, Appuldurcombe House, www.appuldurcombe.co.uk 01983 852484. Daily flying displays, May-Sept, 11am, 1pm, 3pm, Oct-Apr, 11am and 2pm. Schools Birthdays **Open all year** Price B.

Yarmouth(near), Fort Victoria Marine Aquarium, off A3054, www.fortvictoria.co.uk 01983 760283. Discover many creatures found in local waters including seahorses, rays and anemones. Open Easter-Oct, 10am–6pm. Schools Birthdays Price A.

Yaverland, Isle of Wight Zoo, Yaverland Seafront, www.isleofwightzoo.com 01983 403883. This conservation-minded zoo has a Tiger and Big Cat Sanctuary with a rare white tigress. Lemurs, monkeys, reptiles and giant spiders also to view. Open daily, Easter-Oct, 10am-5pm. Schools Price B.

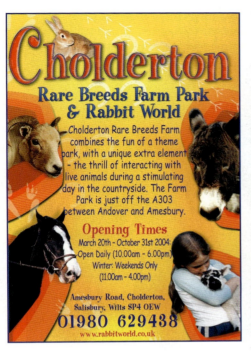

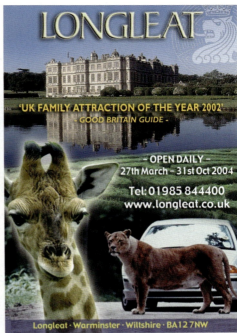

Fun Learning & Activity Holidays for 8 - 17 year olds

Residential or Non-Residential Courses at Lavant House or Slindon College, Sussex

Weekly during July and August

French, German, Spanish

or English as a foreign language

★ Lively International Atmosphere
★ Make friends from many different countries
★ Practise and improve a language naturally
★ On-campus swimming pool, squash, playing fields, Horse-riding, art, drama, cookery, parties, discos etc.
★ Excursions, shopping and sightseeing trips.

Cambridge Language & Activity Courses
10 Shelford Park Avenue, Great Shelford, Cambridge CB2 5LU
Tel: 01223 240340 / 562360 Email: anne@clac.org.uk
www.clac.org.uk

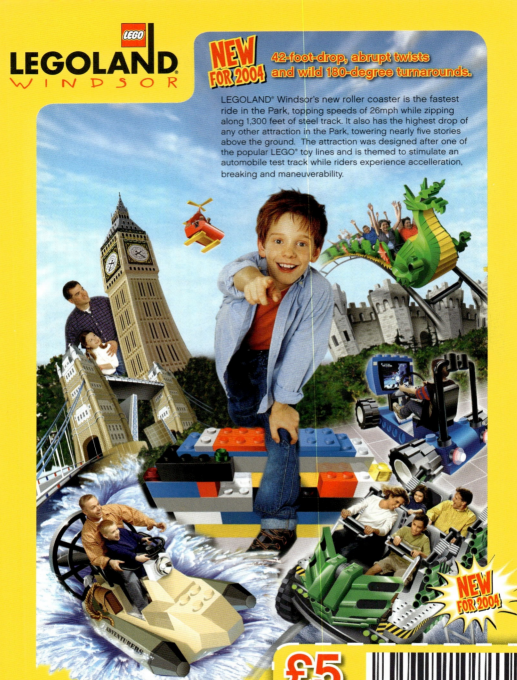

Places to go outside the area

Visit some exciting places just a little further afield.

BERKSHIRE

Windsor, LEGOLAND® www.legoland.co.uk 08705 040404, set in 150 acres of lovely parkland, offers an exciting and imaginative day out with lots of hands-on, interactive discovery. A brand new Jungle Coaster ride for 2004 promises thrills of acceleration, speed and high drops along a wild roller-coaster track that is themed to simulate an automobile test! Exciting experiences await as you wander through the Creation Centre, discover the Imagination Centre, enter LEGO® EXPLORE Land and have a go in the Driving School. Take the younger children to the Waterworks area, watch the daring stunt shows, scale the challenging Climbing Wall, brave the Pirate Falls and explore Miniland, made from over 35 million LEGO® bricks. Open 20th Mar-31st Oct, daily (except some Tues, Wed in Spring & Autumn), from 10am, closing times vary. **Schools Price G Check out page 58.**

SURREY

Guildford, Guildford Spectrum, Parkway www.guildfordspectrum.co.uk 01483 443322. Enjoy the complete leisure experience here! At one exciting venue there is tenpin bowling, an Olympic sized ice-skating rink which is home to the Guildford Flames, four pools, including a leisure pool, a 25m competition pool, teaching pool and diving pool. Other facilities include, a soft play area, laser sports game, health and fitness suite, sports arena and athletics stadium. There is a choice of catering on site and children's holiday activities are organised. Family tickets and special public sessions available. **Check out page 60.**

SUSSEX

Cambridge Language & Activity Courses. CLAC, www.clac.org.uk 01223 240340, organises interesting Summer courses for 8-13 year and 14-17 year olds at two separate sites in lovely countryside locations, Lavant House and Slindon College, West Sussex. The idea is to bring together British and foreign students to create natural language exchange in a motivated and fun environment. There are French, German and Spanish classes for British students and English for overseas students. Fully supervised in a safe environment, there are lots of activities such as swimming, tennis, team games and competitions, drama and music, in addition to the language tuition. Residential or not, these courses offer enjoyable multi-activity weeks with 20 hours of specific tuition in small groups. Courses run weekly during July and August. Please call for more details and a brochure. **Birthdays Check out page 57.**

WILTSHIRE

Warminster, Longleat, off A36, on A362 Warminster to Frome road, www.longleat.co.uk 01985 844400. Voted 'UK Family Attraction of the Year 2002' by 'The Good Britain Guide', Longleat is a great day out for all the family. Discover lions, tigers and giraffe within this world famous safari park before going on to explore the many attractions combined within the Longleat Passport: Longleat House, the World's Longest Hedge Maze, Safari Boats, the Adventure Castle and the Blue Peter Maze, Longleat Railway, Pets Corner, Postman Pat Village and more. A Passport includes one visit to all 12 attractions with the option of returning before the end of the season (31st Oct 2004) to complete any not previously visited. All attractions open daily, 27th Mar-31st Oct. House also open, Sat-Sun & school hols only, 1st Jan-26th Mar; daily, 27th Mar-24th Dec, 26th-31st Dec. **Schools Birthdays Price G Check out page 57.**

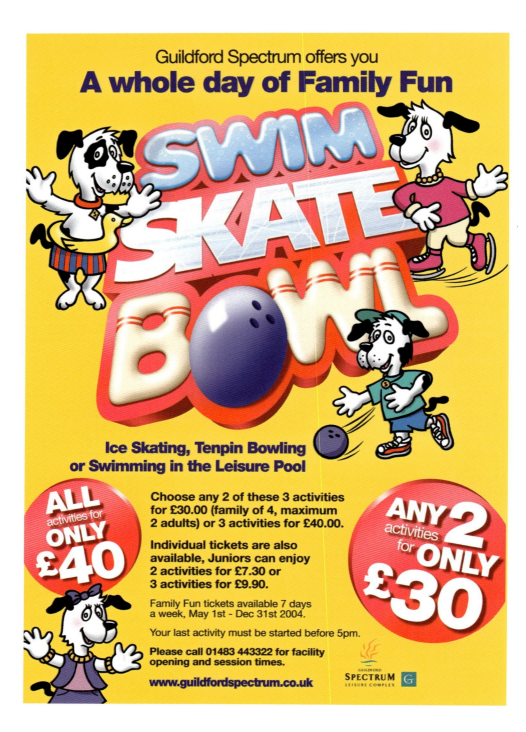

LET'S VISIT LONDON

BBC Television Centre Tours, Wood Lane, Shepherd's Bush, www.bbc.co.uk/tours 0870 6030304. Discover the history, the here and now as well as the digital future, of the most famous TV Centre in the world. Thousands of programmes are produced here every year including favourites such as Top of the Pops, Blue Peter, Parkinson and CBBC. On your tour you are likely to see into studios, visit BBC News, enter into the Top of the Pops Star Bar, play within the interactive studio and much more. Tours run 6 times a day, Mon-Sat and last for up to two hours. Tours are available for anyone over the age of 9 yrs and must be pre-booked. Television Centre is a working building so studio activity on the day of your visit cannot be guaranteed. The nearest Tube Station is White City on the Central Line. **Schools** **Open all year** **Price C**.

The London Aquarium, County Hall, Westminster Bridge Road, www.londonaquarium.co.uk 0207 967 8000 (information) 020 7967 8007 (school bookings). One of Europe's largest displays of aquatic life with over 350 species in over 50 displays, including the huge Pacific and Atlantic tanks. Information on the exciting daily feeds and talks can be found on the activities screen on arrival. Includes the spectacular Atlantic dive, where divers hand feed six foot long conger eels, rays and sharks. Educational tours and literature are available. Open daily, 10am-6pm (extended to 7pm in main holiday periods). Close to Westminster tube and Waterloo tube/mainline stations. **Schools** **Birthdays** **Open all year** **Price C** **Check out page 62.**

London's Transport Museum, Covent Garden Piazza, www.ltmuseum.co.uk 020 7565 7299 (recorded information), 020 7379 6344 (education service), using imaginative and dynamic displays, takes you on a fascinating journey through time and recounts the story of the interaction between transport, the capital and its people from 1800 to the present day. Look out for the under 5s funbus, try the bus and tube simulators, meet characters from the past, see models and working displays and get interactive in the many 'KidZones'. More fun learning than you would have thought possible! Good educational material and lots of special holiday activities. There is now free admission for children under 16. Open daily, 10am-6pm, but 11am-6pm on Fridays. **Schools** **Open all year** **Price B** **Check out page 63.**

LET'S TAKE A TRIP

On the River Thames with City Cruises, www.citycruises.com 02077 400 400. Add excitement for the children, a new perspective for everyone and get excellent value by seeing some of London's best sights from the River Thames aboard a City Cruises luxury river-liner using a River Red Rover ticket! You can travel as far as Greenwich to see the Cutty Sark. For just £8.70 for an adult ticket, £4.35 for a child or just £23 for a family ticket, you can use a hop-on hop-off service between the major destination piers on the River! From Westminster Pier services run every 20 minutes to Tower Pier, and, every 40 minutes to Greenwich via Waterloo and Tower Pier. Your River Red Rover will give you unlimited daily travel between these piers. Admire the Houses of Parliament, Big Ben and the London Eye, see St Paul's Cathedral and look out for the Tate Modern. Lots to see from these super boats with cafe style facilities and a capacity of 520 seats. **Open all year** **Price C** **Check out page 63.**

The Original Tour, London Sightseeing Bus Tours, www.theoriginaltour.com 020 8877 2120, provides a great way to introduce children to the splendid sights of London. The open top buses afford clear uncluttered views from a comfortable seat. You can hop-on and off at over 90 easily accessed stops. Children are both entertained and educated by the special commentary designed for them, as magical stories about London unfold with tales from Roman times until the present day. Listen out for the ghostly 'Spirit of London'. There is an exclusive 'Kids Club' too. The service runs frequently, seven days a week. Times vary seasonally for each route. Every customer is eligible for a free Thames River Cruise! For more information or to enjoy a special discount call 020 8877 2120 or visit www.theoriginaltour.com and quote LGWC. **Open all year** **Price G** **Check out page 63.**

OCEANS OF COLOUR

From sharks, stingrays and piranhas to moray eels, lionfish and sideways walking crabs, London Aquarium is full of surprises with 350 different species to discover.

Located in County Hall, right next to the London Eye, the London Aquarium is just over Westminster Bridge from Big Ben and the Houses of Parliament, and a short walk from Waterloo station.

So, don't plan a day out in London without visiting London's only Aquarium!

Check out our special group, family and school rates.

LONDON AQUARIUM
FLOOD YOUR SENSES

Tel 020 7967 8000   www.londonaquarium.co.uk

Insist on 'The Original'. Live English speaking guides and seven language commentaries.

Exclusive 'Kids Club' includes commentary especially for children and free activity packs

www.theoriginaltour.com
Tel: 020 8877 2120

Web and phone booking discounts - quote LGWC

River Red Rover Ticket

Unlimited daily river travel between Westminster, Waterloo, Tower & Greenwich for just

£8.70 for adults
£4.35 for children
£23 for family tickets

Telephone : 02077 400 400

LET'S PLAY

Snakes and Ladders, Syon Park, Brentford, www.snakes-and-ladders.co.uk 020 8847 0946, is well signposted from Syon Park or can be accessed via 237 or 267 bus from Kew Bridge BR or Gunnersbury Underground Station. Children will find action packed fun whatever the weather. They can let off steam in the giant supervised indoor main play frame, intermediate 2-5s area or toddlers area and use the outdoor adventure playground when the sun shines. A mini motor-bike circuit provides an exciting additional activity, while parents can relax in the cafe overlooking the play frame. Open daily, 10am-6pm. All children must wear socks. Schools Birthdays **Open all year** Price A.

LET'S GO TO A CAFÉ

The Clay Café, 8-10 Monkville Parade, Finchley Road, Temple Fortune, www.theclaycafe.co.uk 020 8905 5353, is an exciting blend of cuisine and entertainment that positively welcomes families with children of all ages. The combination of a full service bistro style restaurant plus a paint-it-yourself ceramic studio offers a fresh and innovative approach to providing creative relaxation for both adults and children alike. Choose from over 200 pieces of pottery (dinnerware, vases, animals etc) and a qualified Art Technician will assist you in creating a unique masterpiece! Glass painting and T-shirt painting are also on offer. Open daily, Mon-Fri, 11am-10pm, Sat, 10am-11pm, Sun, 11am-10pm. Schools Birthdays **Open all year** Prices vary.

The Rainforest Cafe, 20 Shaftesbury Avenue, Piccadilly Circus, www.therainforestcafe.co.uk 020 7434 3111, brings the sights and sounds of a tropical rainforest into a 340-seat restaurant spanning three floors. Foods have wonderfully exciting names and there are many special effects including tropical rain showers, thunder and lightning storms, cascading waterfalls, rainforest mists and the cacophony of wildlife noises! Look out for tropical fish, chattering gorillas, trumpeting elephants, slithering boa and life-sized crocodile! Reservations possible at certain times with the exception of weekends and school holidays. Open Mon-Fri from 12noon, weekends and holidays open from 11.30am. Schools Birthdays **Open all year** Price G **Check out page 66**.

LET'S GO TO THE THEATRE

The Lion King, Lyceum Theatre, Wellington Street, www.disney.co.uk/MusicalTheatre 0870 243 9000 (ticket hotline), 020 7845 0949 (group bookings). One of the most successful Disney films in history, stunningly recreated on stage, is a thrilling and original musical which brings a rich sense of Africa to the stage through a medley of exotic sights and sounds. The show opens in the well loved Disney setting of 'Pride Rock' where 'Simba' the new lion cub is presented to a magical parade of Safari animals. One cannot fail to appreciate the inspiration that allows the giraffes to strut, the birds to swoop and the gazelles to bound. This initial spectacle is breathtaking as the entire savannah comes to life. Wonder at the creativity of the set as the sun rises, savannah plains sway, cattle stampede, drought takes hold and starry skies give up their secrets. Huge variety is offered in the musical score ranging from pulsating African rhythms to contemporary rock. Tim Rice and Elton John's Oscar winning work is unforgettable. A show not to be missed. **Open all year** Price G **Check out page 64.**

The Miz Kids' Club, is an exciting drama experience for children to go behind the scenes of the brilliant musical, Les Misérables, and to enjoy a matinee performance of the show. This is a great opportunity for children to enter the world of theatre and discover the fascination of a big West End production. Back stage, children see the costumes and props, hear the story of Les Misérables, learn one of the famous songs, join in drama games and improvise a key scene. Older children look at the technical operation of the stage effects and focus on characterisation in their improvisation workshop. The clubs meet before the Saturday matinee at 10.30am for 8–11s and 10.45am for 12–15s, both finishing at 1.15pm. Packages, from £23, include a CD synopsis of Les Misérables, sent in advance of their visit, a snack packed lunch and a ticket to the performance on the day. For details visit www.lesmis.com or call 020 7439 3062. **Open all year Check out page 64.**

LGWTC

A WILD PLACE TO SHOP AND EAT®

Combine animated wildlife and special effects. Add phenomenal food made from the freshest ingredients and you've captured the breathtaking, dynamic features that embody Rainforest Cafe.

FREE
SMOOTHIE OR DESSERT

With every main course ordered by your party

020 7434 3111

20 Shaftesbury Avenue, Piccadilly Circus, London W1D 7EU
www.therainforestcafe.co.uk

Please present to your safari guide when seated.
Cannot be used in conjunction with any other offer.

Index

Abbotsbury Swannery. 49
Adventure Activities 31
Airborne Forces Museum 24
Aldershot Military Museum 24
Alice in Wonderland Family Park 13
Amazon World Zoo Park. 56
Andover Museums 43
Appuldurcombe House 30
Aquadrome 15
Avon Beach 40,42
Badger and Wildlife Watch 49
Balloon Rides 31
Basing House 24
Beachside Leisure Centre 15
Bembridge Windmill 22,29
Bicycle Hire 7
Birdworld and Underwater World 53
Bishops Waltham Palace 24
Blackgang Chine 19
Blue Boat Trips 6,9
Blue Pool 50
Blue Reef Aquarium 55
Boat Hire 7
Boat Trips & Ferry Services 8
Bournemouth Aviation Museum 21
Bowling (Ten Pin) 31
Brading Roman Villa 29
Branstone Farm Studies Centre 56
Brass Rubbing 32
Breamore House and Countryside Museum 25
Brewers Quay 42
Brickfields Horse Country 55
Broadlands 26
Brownsea Island 49
Bursledon Windmill 25
Bus Trips 11
Butser Ancient Farm 26
Butterfly World and Fountain World. 56
Calbourne Water Mill and Rural Museum. 29
Calshot Castle 25
Cambridge Language & Activity Courses 57,59
Carisbrooke Castle 29
Cavalcade of Costume 21
Charles Dickens Birthplace 26
Charmouth Heritage Coast Centre 49
Children's Action Farm 53
Children's Farm and Smugglers Barn 49
Cholderton Rare Breeds Farm Park 55,57
Cinemas 32
Classic Boat Museum 30
Climbing Centre (Indoor) 32
Coastal Visitors Centre 30
Colemans Animal Farm. 56
Compton Acres 50
Corfe Castle 23
Crazy Golf 32
Cumberland House. 27
D-Day Museum 27
Deep Sea Adventure and Sharky's 13
Dinosaur Farm Museum 55
Dinosaur Isle 22,30
Dinosaurland 23
Dinosaur Museum 23
Discover Salisbury. 28
Discovery 23
Dorset County Museum 23
Eling Tide Mill 27
Exbury Gardens 51
EXPLOSION! 25
Face Place 40
Farmer Giles Farmstead. 55
Farmer Palmer's Farm Park 50
Farnborough Air Sciences Museum 44
Finkley Down Farm Park. 48,51
Flamingo Park Wildlife Encounter 56
Fort Brockhurst. 25
Fort Victoria Marine Aquarium 56
Fossil Hunting 33
Free Places 41
Funny Farm 13
Gilbert White's House and Garden and the Oates Museum 27
Grease On Tour 37,38
Guildford Spectrum. 59,60
Gurkha Museum. 27
Hampshire Mega Maze 14,15
Havant Museum. 44
Haven House Visitor Centre. 53
Hawk Conservancy 55
Hawthorns Urban Wildlife Centre 40,44
Headhunters Laser Combat. 19
Heritage Centre 29
Highclere Castle 26
Highcliffe Castle 21
Hillier Gardens, Sir Harold. 51
Historic Dockyard. 26
Hollycombe Steam Collection. 14,17
Honeybrook Farm. 50
Horse-Drawn Trips 11
Hurst Castle 25
Ice Skating 33
Intech 27
Island Planetarium 30
Isle of Wight Bus and Coach Museum . . . 30
Isle of Wight Model Railways. 29
Isle of Wight Shipwreck Centre 29
Isle of Wight Wax Works 29
Isle of Wight Zoo 56
Itchen Valley Country Park 45,47
Jane Austen's House 25
Jo Jingles. 33,34
Karting 33
Keep Military Museum 23
King John's House. 26
Kingcombe Centre 50
Kingston Lacy House and Park. 24
Kingston Maurward Gardens. 49
Larmer Tree Gardens 55
LEGOLAND®. 58,59
Leisureranch. 15
Lilliput Antique Doll and Toy Museum 29
Local Councils 4
London Attractions. 61
Longbridge Mill. 44
Longdown Activity Farm 51,54
Longleat 57,59
Lulworth Castle 23
Lyme Regis Marine Aquarium and Cobb History. . . 50
Lymington Open Air Sea Water Pool. 34,37
Manor Farm. 51

Maritime Museum	25
Marwell Zoological Park	52,53
Matchams Leisure Park	17
Medieval Merchants House	27
Mid-Hants Watercress Line	12
Milestones	22,24
Model Railway	30
Model Village	29
Mompesson House	28
Monkey Music	33,34
Monkey World	48,50
Morton Manor	29
Mottisfont Abbey	22,26
Mottistone Manor Garden	22,55
Museum of Army Flying and Explorers' World	25
Museum of Electricity	21
Museum of Island History	30
Music and Movement	33
National Motor Museum	24
National Trust	22
Natural History Centre	29
Needles Old Battery	22,29
Needles Park	19
New Barn Field Centre	21
New Forest Otter, Owl and Wildlife Conservation Park	51,54
New Forest Museum and Visitor Centre	25
New Forest Reptile Centre	44
Newport Ghost Walk	30
Nostalgia Toy Museum	29
Nothe Fort	24
Oceanarium	49
Old Sarum	28
Old Town Hall & Nature Reserve	22,30
Old Wardour Castle	28
Osborne House	29
Outburst, Salisbury	19
Owl and Falconry Centre	56
Party Idea	33
Paultons Park	16,17
Pitch and Putt	33
Playzone	14,17
Porchester Castle	26
Portland Castle	23
Portsmouth City Museum and Records Office	33,34
Pottery Café	33,34
Pottery Painting	33
Priest's House Museum and Garden	24
Putlake Adventure Farm	50
Putting Greens	35
Pyramids Centre	18
Quad Biking	35
Quasar	13
Redcoats in The Wardrobe Museum	28
Red House Museum and Gardens	21
RNLI Headquarters	42
Robin Hill	19
Rockbourne Roman Villa	26
Roman Villa	30
Romsey Rapids	17
Royal Green Jackets Museum	28
Royal Marines Museum	27
Royal Navy Submarine Museum	25
Royal Signals Museum	21
Royal Victoria Country Park	26
RSPB Reserve	42
Run-About	15
Rushmoor Leisure Services	4
Russell-Cotes Art Gallery and Museum	41
St Barbe Museum and Art Gallery	25
Salisbury Cathedral	46
Salisbury and South Wiltshire Museum	28
Sammy Miller Museum	26
Sandown Rides	19
Scaplen's Court Museum	28
Serendipity Sam's (3 venues)	13,17,18
Shanklin Chine	56
Sherborne Castle	23
Sherborne Old Castle	23
Skateboarding	35
Smuggling Museum	30
Snowsports	35
Southampton Museums and Attractions	45
Southsea Attractions	27
Southsea Castle	27
Space Ace	15
Splashdown	13
Sporting and Arts Events	35
Sports and Leisure Centres	36
SS Shieldhall	45
Stagecoach South East	6,11
Stapehill Abbey	50
Staunton Country Park	48,53
Stonehenge	28
Stratfield Saye House	27
Sub Tropical Gardens	49
Swanage Lifeboat Station	42
Swanage Railway	11,12
Swimming Pools	36
Tank Driving	11
Tank Museum	21
Teddy Bear House	23
Theatres	37
Timewalk	24
Totton and Eling Heritage Centre	45
Tourist Information Centres	4
Train Trips	11
Treehouse	15
Tutankhamun Exhibition	23
UK Llamas	49
Vyne, The	22,27
Watersports	39
Wellington Country Park	53,54
Westgate Museum	46
Weymouth Sea Life Park	50
Whitchurch Silk Mill	27
Wightlink Isle of Wight Ferries	8
Wilton Carpet Factory	28
Wilton House	28
Wilts & Dorset Buses	10,11
Wimborne Minster Model Town	24
Winchester Attractions	45
Winchester City Mill	22,28
Worldlife and the Lullingstone Silk Farm	50
Yarmouth Castle	30
Youth Hostelling	39,40